The Selected Writings of Salvatore Quasimodo

EDITED AND TRANSLATED FROM THE ITALIAN BY Allen Mandelbaum

MINERVA PRESS

Library of Congress Catalog Card Number: 60-9231

Minerva Press edition published in 1968
by arrangement with Farrar, Straus & Giroux, Inc.

Funk & Wagnalls, A Division of *Reader's Digest Books, Inc.*

Printed in the United States of America

CONTENTS

The page numbers after the poem titles refer to the English translation. The Italian text is on the facing page.

ERATO AND APOLLYON [1932–1936]

SUNKEN OBOE [1930–1932]

Day after day, [1943–1946]

Life is not dream, [1946–1948]

The false and true green, [1949–1955]

The incomparable earth, [1955–1958]

A note on this translation

It was eight years ago that Renato Poggioli first suggested I translate a group of poems by Salvatore Quasimodo. That early exercise matured through difficult years to more ambitious dimensions: a triad of volumes that would make available to English readers the three presences that have contributed most to this half century of Italian poetry—Giuseppe Ungaretti, Eugenio Montale, and Quasimodo. Each volume was to be ample enough to escape the cursoriness of an anthology, to permit a full encounter. Yet if I wanted the poetic encounter to take place one by one, the critical encounter was less easy to handle in separate volumes. Thus, the reader who approaches Quasimodo can be referred with some profit to my brief introduction to the volume on Ungaretti that appeared in 1958, and to the essay that bears the title "Quasimodo" (*Inventario*, May–December 1954) where I have dealt with all three poets, and attempted particularly to distinguish the voice of Quasimodo from that of his elder, Ungaretti, with whom Italian critics have too easily confounded him.

In the following pages, it is Quasimodo who speaks for himself as critic in the two essays that have been included. Both are polemical and—in the light of the poetry, where Quasimodo can often be too nostalgic for the prophetic power he would summon, too elegiac for the nightmare he would comprehend—programmatic. But the statements form part of a whole of a body of work where person and poet stand tenaciously together, and where intentions form a vital part of that stance. The first essay, "Discorso sulla poesia," can now be found at the end of *Il falso e vero verde*, 1956, in the Mondadori edition of that volume; the second, "Dante," first appeared in *Inventario* (January–April 1954).

For the poetic of translation that presides over this volume, the briefest word: The freedom and necessity that inhabit one's own poetry are less present in translating. There, "I can" (with its hint of bravado) can usurp the only rightful emblem of the poet, "I must." It is out of my desire to temper that "I can" that these translations bear with them—like most fidelities—as much respect as love. The question I have addressed to myself was not "How should I have written this?" but "How should I wish to be translated?", and literal exigencies have been uppermost.

The text I have followed is that of the standard Mondadori edition, in five volumes. The first of these, *Ed è subito sera*, 1942, is an omnibus volume that contains, in reverse chronological order, Quasimodo's earlier books: *Erato e Apòllion*, 1936; *Òboe sommerso*, 1932; and *Acque e terre*, 1930. The one hundred poems chosen were drawn from a total of one hundred seventy in the five Mondadori volumes; the course of Quasimodo's work from the early "Hermetic" season through the later "public" poetry is, thus, substantially available here, with few—if any—significant omissions.

For the presence of Quasimodo, I have been grateful, as for that of Marjorie Bogat, M. T. Grendi, and Fernando Basso.

A. M.

Cassino
March 1960

SQ

Discourse on poetry

Philosophers—the natural enemies of poets—and those who steadily catalogue critical thought, assert that poetry (and all the arts), like the works of nature, undergoes no changes during or after a war. An illusion, because war alters the moral life of a people. Man, at his return from war, no longer finds measures of certainty in an inner *modus* of life, a *modus* he has forgotten or treated ironically during his trials with death.

War summons up, with violence, a hidden order in the thought of man, a greater grasp of the truth: the occasions of reality inscribe themselves in its history. Valéry, in 1918, closes a period of French poetry, and Apollinaire begins another, the modern period. The sway of D'Annunzio (and it was he who had sounded the call to arms) crumbles in that same year, and there begins the reaction against his poetry, his diction. In 1945, silence insinuates itself into the Hermetic school of Italian poetry. Since then, critics have begun to put the so-called "time of waiting" on trial. Does the most recent chapter of Italian poetry represent the maturity or the decadence of a language? Criticism cannot answer; and it tries to draw up balance sheets or pseudo-histories of poetry between the two wars, indicating its relations with a humanist tradition. These are provisional tombstones that will be lifted one day when the chronicle of formal ashes gives way to the history of contemporary poetic man. Grown arid in a method that is too abstract or too "methodological," a portion of criticism has—for more than twenty years—called on "taste" to recognize or deny what is poetry. More steeped in Romantic vices than it was aware, it attached itself to "forms," believing it had thus evaded Crocean criticism. By means of judicious deformations (the false scheme of "literary generations," for example), a recent anthology of twentieth-century Italian poetry presents us with a waxwork museum—from 1905 to 1945—in which several figures (from the *Crepuscolari*—the poets of the Twilight School—to the heads and tails of the Hermetic school) are arranged in a sequence that has a purely verbal life, without any systematic base. It seems to me that Hermetic criticism began its first exercises in reading around 1936 with a study by Oreste Macrì on the "poetic of the word" in my poetry. The philosopher demonstrated his enthusiasm for a philological method; perhaps that was the right way, following the lesson of history, to arrive at some conclusions about the origins of the Italian poetic language of today. Another critic, Luciano Anceschi, the anthologist noted above, followed the lessons of his teacher, Giuseppe De Robertis, in attributing to Dino Campana and then to the Twilight poets the first revolts against D'Annunzio and the first timid utterances of a new *ars poetica.* All this, in order to bring the innovations of Ungaretti (of *L'Allegria*, be it understood, which is not yet a Hermetic volume) into line with tradition. From premises such as these, a hazy, baroque perspective leads the critic to unsteady judgments, to bewildering documents on the validity of a poetic period in Italian literary history that is concrete and positive. One cannot deny that there was, indeed, a Hermetic school; but the critic who tried, ambitiously, to inquire into the innovators, instead of presenting a "semantic of constructions" (i.e., of images) in order to establish the origins of that school, has gone back to the abstract geometry of pure art, to an Arcadia. Evident here is the absence of any critical orientation towards recent poetry, that poetry crystallized by the last war; while other minor critics turned against the silence of the poets with new symbolisms and existential pronouncements. Has all this meant a criticism by means of emblems? A purely formal criticism? The results fade away in approximations. Here the Twilight poets, there the Futurists, and there again the poets of *La Voce;* a chronicle that cannot distinguish poetry from literature. The Hermetic poets, in fact, make their appearance as ascertainable motifs of a literary movement. They continue a phase that had been interrupted in the years before 1918 by the "shadow" Sergio Corazzini, the phantom Dino Campana, the hobgoblin Camillo Sbarbaro (these epithets only reflect the unsolidity of the images that critics portray). And when, in dealing with the poets between the wars, the critics present us, not with men but phantoms—they can only remind us that too many centuries of Italian poetry carry the precious echoes of Arcadia, voices quenched by the Communes, the Signorias, the Princely States, the Courts, the ecclesiastical powers. This is the heritage of conventional encounters, where the poet is the "unloved lover" with platitudes—from fire to ice—that are as punctual as death. The image of the poet that would emerge from this: a man of sentimental risks, a lesser nature suspended in love—love that all others, except him, possess. This is the aesthetic and doctrinaire image that would rescue, from the origins of Italian literature until today, seven or eight poets, seven or eight men. Because it is so faithful to traditional operations (dealing always, except for two or three adequate and communicable examples, in the narrow range of a literary—not a poetic—voice), this criticism can only give rise, if anything, to a question: Who are these poets, and what do they represent in the contemporary world? Do they toy with shadows in pure forms or, rather, do they join life and literature through the growth of their awareness and their response to the pressures of time?

The critical itinerary is necessary. The last war overtook a poetic language that was drawing near to the objects of the earth in order to reach the universal. Allegories had been dissolved in the solitude of the dictatorship. But criticism preferred to resolve the poetic process in intellectual terms: it believed that one could single out poetic personalities, the existence of the shaping word, in symbols and in Petrarchesque, baroque gyrations. But where literature "reflects," poetry "makes." The poet participates in literature only *after* his experience as an "irregular." The poet shatters, both naturally and unnaturally, a metrical and technical habit, and modifies the world with his freedom and truth. The voice of Homer exists before Greece, and Homer "forms" the civilization of Greece. Even a complete "history of forms as the history of the word" does not, then, exhaust the history of the poets. The poet is a man who is linked to other men in the field of culture and is important for his "content" (that is the grave word) not only for his voice, his cadence (immediately recognizable when it is imitated).

The poet does not "say"; he sums up his own soul and consciousness and makes these—his secrets—"exist," forcing them out of anonymity into personality. What, then, are the words of these poets between the two wars? Are these poets masters, who have a right to citizenship in the contemporary world, or are they rather pilgrims, only engaged in stylistic operations, worn-out literary categories? No one has answered this question, and the critics (many between the two wars) have repeated unspecific schemes, and given us facsimiles rather than images of men. Poetry is the man, as I have said: and the filing cards enumerated by "taste" are barely an introduction to the drama of a part of Italian history, only notes to be developed. The logic of the fantasy, as criticism, cannot confront poetry, because poetry does not "measure" good inventions; its responsibility is not to falsehood but to truth.

In 1945, alongside formalist criticism, that had been empirical, wavering, unsure of itself in making judgments, there emerged, even if in limited form, a realist criticism, not yet Marxist, but tending towards the orthodox formulation of that doctrine. The history of poetry between the two wars, which had remained in the encyclopedic "limbo" of varied aesthetic tendencies, descended now to other and more scientific scrutiny. We know how risky is the theoretical machinery of an aesthetic before it is systematized; and the Marxist aesthetic, too, is in a phase of development, making use of the writings of Marx and Engels on art and literature that have to be interpreted in the light of the growth of contemporary critical thought. But from a new conception of the world, we have the right to expect inquiries that are more aware of the presence of man.

From 1945 on, and always for the historical reasons indicated earlier, the new generation, reacting against existing poetics, found itself unexpectedly without any apparent masters for the continued writing of poetry. This generation refused the humanist tradition—recognizing the maturity but not the finality of that tradition—and gave rise to a literary situation that can only excite admiration in those who are interested in the fate of Italian culture. The search for a new poetic language coincides this time with an impetuous search for man: in substance, the reconstruction of man defrauded by war, that "remaking of man" to which I referred, precisely in 1946, but not in a moralistic sense, because morals cannot constitute poetry. A new poetic language, when another is about to reach its maturity (as was the case in 1945 with the language of the Hermetic poets), necessarily involves an extreme violence. Formalist criticism (and not only this), faced with the poetic documents of the new generation, speaks disparagingly of a "translation style," considering the desire for "discourse" of the postwar poets only in its external aspects (at times ametrical and prosaic).

But does the "translation style" have no native origins, does it mean the imitation of foreign spirits and poetics? This is a point to be made clear. In reaction against the traditional Italian Arcadia, the contaminated elegiac amorous exercises, the reborn Petrarchism, there emerges the first lexicon of a new poetry, whose syntactic efforts include spacious rhythms and "forms" (the lexicon of the poetry between the wars had already been made specific, through rigorous inquiry, by Francesco Flora). This may involve mistaken hexameters, that answer to the "presumption" of a literary genre. But we are witnessing the growth of a social poetry, that addresses itself to the various aggregates of human society. Not, of course, sociological poetry, because no poet dreams of invoking his soul and his intelligence to fashion "sociological theory." Dante, Petrarch, Foscolo, Leopardi wrote social poems, poems necessary at a given moment of civilization. But the poetry of the new generation, which we shall call social in the sense indicated above, aspires to dialogue rather than monologue. It is already a demand for dramatic poetry, an elementary "form" of theater. (In the same way, the *Con-*

trasto of Ciullo d'Alcamo and the *Lamenti* of the Sicilian school marked a breaking-away from the Provençal school, which—except for a few poets—was another Arcadia.) The new poetry may become dramatic or epic (in a modern sense) but not, I repeat, gnomic or sociological. Civil poetry, one knows, is beset by deep traps, and sometimes it has toyed with "estheticisms." Remember Tyrtaeus, who invites the youths to fight in the front ranks for their homeland, because the cadaver of an old man is ugly, while the body of a dead boy is always beautiful. The new generation is truly *engagé* in every sense in the literary field. The new "contents" are heavy at times, but the content is conditioned by the course of history. The poet knows today that he cannot write idylls or horoscopes. Fortunately, he is not beset by critics alongside him indicating more or less probable outcomes for poetry, as happened between the two wars: a criticism that anticipates poetic solutions, a philosophy become the master of poetry. Hegel wrote that art was dying because it was being resolved into philosophy, that is, into thought: and today it may seem that poetry tends to disappear in the "thought" of poetry.

Returning now to that "translation style," the term used with contempt to indicate the texture of poetry around 1945, let us note that both formalist criticism as well as historical materialist criticism intended by that a language drawn directly from the translation of a poetic text from a foreign language. Was this term accurate or was it not, rather, a loose formulation by critics when faced with a "taste" for speaking of the world and the things of this world that used a new technique, prelude to a concrete language that reflects the real and disturbs the traditional planes of rhetoric? Our poetic tradition has always seemed to the foreign reader to be layer on thick layer of impenetrable schemes, in which man spends his precious time in elegiac occasions, detached from the authentic passions intrinsic to his nature. After forty years of critical silence about Italian poetry, Europe has again begun to read our poetic manuscripts; not those poems that mime the Hermetic school, but those that answer or pose questions to men, the poems of '43, '44, '45 and of dates even closer to us. Is this interest owing only to a projection of sentiments and objects common to the man of today? Is it, then, an attention of an ethical and problematic nature? I do not believe so: it is precisely the "formal reasons," those least apparent now to us, that make our poetry participate humanly in the world. Our poetry gains attention not because of its linguistic exercises, but because of its poetic responsibilities, those that had been obscured after Leopardi. It is the sign of an active presence of our civilization and—with it—of Italian man (this, the true tradition, beyond the courtly flutes of nature subdued in a perennial Arcadia).

The secret of a poetic language reveals itself late to criticism; that is, when the model has already branched out into imitation, when its best memory falls to fragments, becomes a "school." It is then that minor poets propose, in guise of beauty, well-balanced literary mannerisms, superimposed on the repetition of "common" images, no longer original. Can man, as he is, be the content of a rigidly deterministic poetic? In describing the poetic experience of these past years, some have spoken of "ethical realism," with the "real" (or the truth) referring to what is represented, and the "ethical" to the aim of the representation. It is easy to catalogue; but man's precarious existence, the harshness of his political mind, his struggle against pain—all have brought man near to man and the poet to his listener. At times the modern poet is eloquent (ancient hortatory eloquence has a different metaphorical voice); he seems, that is, to discourse with a world gathered up in a narrow landscape (the poet's own land): eloquent, even if the tone of his voice is subdued, familiar. These poets are often men of Southern Italy—of Lucania, Abruzzo, Puglia, the islands—but also of Piedmont, of Veneto. Their inheritance was close-to-the earth and feudal; erect and clear, they have opened a dialogue on their fate. They have no childhood, or memory of childhood, only chains to burst and concrete realities with which to enter the cultural life of the nation. The muses of the woods and valleys are silent in them: their peasant mythologies are filled, rather, with the roar of landslides and floods. One day we shall chart a geographical map of the South; and it matters not if it will still touch Magna Grecia, whose sky extends over imperturbable images of innocence and blinding senses. There, perhaps, the "permanence" of poetry is being born. Luckily, those regions have no "lettered" dialect poets to reduce them to the brief space of a vignette, and their syntactic and linguistic "migrations" already carry a particular lexicon, the announcement of a language.

In Tuscany, unfortunately, one can still find some Guittone d'Arezzo, who schools in his precious doctrine the last chimeras of the realms of the absent beloved, where the existential lathe still turns. But in that other poetic and popular geography (though the critics still grant it little space) the presence of man—his gestures, his works—is constant. We shall not speak of ethical realism: the poets only teach us to live: shaping the material into new forms is difficult enough. It took a generation to meditate then carry out the impulse to break up and reconstruct the hendecasyllabic measure. And this, after the accidental loss of the faculty of rhythmic reading, in accord with the traditional metric writing. Poets are recognized by their particular pronunciation of metrical measures, and their voice (their song, we should say) consists of that cadence. The unit of their expression can, prosodically, be long or short; that "voice" will be revealed in any structure. We have a voice for every poet; and in that "translation style," too, what counts is the poetic pronunciation.

Speaking of the language of the "real," in an essay of mine on Dante, I recalled the enduring force of the "simple style." This was also a reference to its intensity, because the language of the *Comedy*, though it had its origins in the *dolce stil nuovo*, was purified through its contact with human and concrete contents. Dante's figures aimed at a drama that was no longer that of the classic world, although his mode of representing or inventing his figures had its roots in the classics. The lesson of Dante served Petrarch and the major writers of the Cinquecento; it was truly a lofty sign of Italian literary civilization. And today it is not only in one direction that we can read Dante in order to forget Petrarch and his obsessive cadences mirrored in the little space assigned to them by the feelings.

Is the social poetry of Dante, his other world so firmly set in the landscape of this earth, still subject to doubt, or can it be the "legal" point of departure for the new poets? The "translation" style can surprise anyone who is accustomed to the traditional movement of the lyric; but it begins a discourse that is unusual in Italian poetry, shattering forever the harmonious approaches to Arcadias. It may well create other rhetorics, but it will draw our poetry out from bondage, our poetry that has but recently entered the literary domain of European man, blocked off as it was, till yesterday, by walls of silence: the same walls that Italian criticism has raised around this poetry. Beyond them, at times, criticism seeks the major figures of the new tendency, using antiquated aesthetic yardsticks (not all, however), and only recognizes "contents," judgments, hopes. Dreams are but the sounds of life, cruel answers to the most frequent and disturbing questions. And forms? Where now is the "*dolce color d'oriëntal zaffiro*" ("sweet hue of oriental sapphire"), "*la fresca aura dei lauri*" ("the cool air of the laurels")?

The two criticisms—formalist and historical materialist—theorize and would create the poets in accord with the limits of their ideas on art. They hope to reduce poetry to a science; but they know it will be the poet, then, to force their science to yield to his rôle of an "irregular."

The motives of my discourse may seem polemical—with reference, too, to my own poetic situation—but the critical documents we now have for the future literary history of the twentieth century in Italy are mediocre witnesses, catalogues of literary artisanship. Poets—I cite the words of Croce—"are little disposed to organic and philosophical consideration, but are acute and subtle in particular questions." They can, then, discuss the examples cited by anthologists and discriminate, if nothing else, between literature and truth; i.e., between literature and poetic creation. And they can consider the figure of the poet in the contemporary world, in his attempt to join life to literature. The relation life-art is at the center of the problems of modern thought: but the supreme aesthetic orders repulse the poet (whom I have called elsewhere "the imperfection of nature") precisely because he has begun a dialogue with man.

"*Chiare, fresche, dolci acque!*" ("Clear, cool, sweet waters!") Would this were a time of such tender utterances, a time in which memory would allow a poetic active enough to re-see the world in its gentle measures and sentiments. But here, now, the present generation, that dares to read new numbers in the tables of poetry, learns day by day what it means to write verses—so simple before the civil and political struggles. Gramsci saw clearly from the darkness of his prison the "literary" principles of the world. The position of the poet cannot be passive in society; he "modifies" the world, as we have said. His forceful images, those that he creates, beat on the heart of man more than does philosophy or history. Poetry is transformed into ethic, precisely because of its beauty: its responsibility is in direct proportion to its perfection. To write verses means to undergo judgment: and implicit in the aesthetic judgment are the social reactions to which a poem gives rise. We know the reservations one must make on these statements. Yet a poet is a poet when he does not renounce his presence in a given land, at a precise time, politically defined. And poetry is the freedom and truth of that time and not the abstract modulations of sentiment.

For criticism to put the works of the "time of waiting" on trial now, in a formative period like the present, is absurd, especially when new aesthetic theories are on the horizon and the continuation of a worn-out poetic school can only give us a false sense of "enduring." War has interrupted a culture and proposed new values for man; and though the weapons have been laid aside, the dialogue of the poets with men is necessary, even more than the sciences and the agreements between nations, which can be betrayed. Italian poetry after 1945 is—in its kind—of a choral nature. It flows with spacious rhythms, speaks of the real world with ordinary words; sometimes it presumes to the epic. It has a difficult fate because it has opened itself to forms that negate the false Italian tradition. Its poets now pay out their silence amid political alarms and the chronicles of moral decadence.

And suddenly it's evening

[1920–1942]

NEW POEMS

[1936–1942]

Ride la gazza, nera sugli aranci

Forse è un segno vero della vita:
intorno a me fanciulli con leggeri
moti del capo danzano in un gioco
di cadenze e di voci lungo il prato
della chiesa. Pietà della sera, ombre
riaccese sopra l'erba cosí verde,
bellissime nel fuoco della luna!
Memoria vi concede breve sonno;
ora, destatevi. Ecco, scroscia il pozzo
per la prima marea. Questa è l'ora:
non piú mia, arsi, remoti simulacri.
E tu vento del sud forte di zàgare,
spingi la luna dove nudi dormono
fanciulli, forza il puledro sui campi
umidi d'orme di cavalle, apri
il mare, alza le nuvole dagli alberi:
già l'airone s'avanza verso l'acqua
e fiuta lento il fango tra le spine,
ride la gazza, nera sugli aranci.

The Magpie Laughs, Black Upon the Orange Trees

Perhaps it is a very sign of life:
around me, children in a game
of cadences and voices dance
with easy movements of the head
along the meadow of the church.
Piety of evening, shadows
rekindled on the grass so green,
loveliest in fire of the moon!
Memory grants you brief sleep;
but now, awake. Behold, the well
churns for the first tide. This is
the hour. Mine no longer, burnt
and distant semblances. And you,
south wind thick with orange blossoms,
drive the moon where children sleep
naked, force the foal to fields
damp with the tracks of mares, bare
the sea, lift the clouds from the trees.
The heron now moves waterward
and slowly sniffs the mud among the thorns;
the magpie laughs, black upon the orange trees.

Strada di Agrigentum

Là dura un vento che ricordo acceso
nelle criniere dei cavalli obliqui
in corsa lungo le pianure, vento
che macchia e rode l'arenaria e il cuore
dei telamoni lugubri, riversi
sopra l'erba. Anima antica, grigia
di rancori, torni a quel vento, annusi
il delicato muschio che riveste
i giganti sospinti giú dal cielo.
Come sola allo spazio che ti resta!
E piú t'accori s'odi ancora il suono
che s'allontana largo verso il mare
dove Èspero già striscia mattutino:
il marranzano tristemente vibra
nella gola al carraio che risale
il colle nitido di luna, lento
tra il murmure d'ulivi saraceni.

Street of Agrigentum

There a wind endures that I recall
kindled in the horses' manes, slanting
in races across the plains, a wind that stains
and wears away the sandstone and the heart
of mournful telamones, overturned
on the grass. Ancient soul, now grey
with rancour, with this wind do you return
to sniff the delicate moss that cloaks the giants
downward thrust from heaven. How alone
you are within the space still left to you!
And more you grieve one hears again the sound
that moves far off and broadly towards the sea,
where Hesperus already creeps with morning:
the marranzano quivers sorrowfully
in the throat of the waggoner, who climbs
the hillside neat beneath the moonlight, slowly
amid the murmur of saracen olive trees.

l. 14: The marranzano is a musical instrument, similar to the jews'-harp, used in Sicily.

La dolce collina

Lontani uccelli aperti nella sera
tremano sul fiume. E la pioggia insiste
e il sibilo dei pioppi illuminati
dal vento. Come ogni cosa remota
ritorni nella mente. Il verde lieve
della tua veste è qui fra le piante
arse dai fulmini dove s'innalza
la dolce collina d'Ardenno e s'ode
il nibbio sui ventagli di saggina.

Forse in quel volo a spirali serrate
s'affidava il mio deluso ritorno,
l'asprezza, la vinta pietà cristiana,
e questa pena nuda di dolore.
Hai un fiore di corallo sui capelli.
Ma il tuo viso è un'ombra che non muta;
(cosí fa morte). Dalle scure case
del tuo borgo ascolto l'Adda e la pioggia,
o forse un fremere di passi umani,
fra le tenere canne delle rive.

The Gentle Hill

Birds far-off and open in the evening
tremble on the river. And the rain insists
and the hissing of the poplars illumined
by the wind. Like everything remote
do you return to mind. The light green
of your dress is here among the plants
burnt by lightning flashes where the gentle
hill of Ardenno rises and one hears
the kite hawk on the fans of broomcorn.

Perhaps in my return deluded, I
confided in that flight of locked-in spirals,
the harshness, the defeated Christian pity,
and this naked pain of sadnesses.
You have a flower of coral in your hair.
But your face is an unchanging shadow;
(thus death does). From the darkened houses
of your borough, I hear the Adda and the rain,
or perhaps a quivering of human steps
upon the banks among the tender canes.

Già la pioggia è con noi

Già la pioggia è con noi,
scuote l'aria silenziosa.
Le rondini sfiorano le acque spente
presso i laghetti lombardi,
volano come gabbiani sui piccoli pesci;
il fieno odora oltre i recinti degli orti.

Ancora un anno è bruciato,
senza un lamento, senza un grido
levato a vincere d'improvviso un giorno.

The Rain's Already With Us

The rain's already with us
tossing silent air.
The swallows skim spent waters
on the Lombard lakes,
fly like gulls at little fish;
beyond the garden enclosures, the scent of hay.

Again a year is burned,
without lament, without a cry
upraised to win us—suddenly—a day.

L'alto veliero

Quando vennero uccelli a muovere foglie
degli alberi amari lungo la mia casa,
(erano ciechi volatili notturni
che foravano i nidi sulle scorze)
io misi la fronte alla luna,
e vidi un alto veliero.

A ciglio dell'isola il mare era sale;
e s'era distesa la terra e antiche
conchiglie lucevano fitte ai macigni
sulla rada di nani limoni.

E dissi all'amata che in sé agitava un mio figlio,
e aveva per esso continuo il mare nell'anima:
« Io sono stanco di tutte quest'ali che battono
a tempo di remo, e delle civette
che fanno il lamento dei cani
quando è vento di luna ai canneti.
Io voglio partire, voglio lasciare quest'isola.»
Ed essa: « O caro, è tardi: restiamo.»

Allora mi misi lentamente a contare
i forti riflessi d'acqua marina
che l'aria mi portava sugli occhi
dal volume dell'alto veliero.

The Tall Schooner

When birds came to stir the leaves
of the bitter trees beside my house
(blind nocturnal birds
boring their nests in the barks)
I faced the moon,
and saw a tall schooner.

At the island's rim the sea was salt;
the earth extended, ancient conches
glittered thrust into the rocks
on the roadstead of dwarf lemon trees.

And I told my love (my child was stirring in her,
and, for that, she had the sea within her soul continuously):
"I'm tired of all these wings that beat
in time to oars, and of the owls
that howl a dog's lament
when wind of moon is in the cane brakes.
I want to leave, I want to leave this island."
And she: "O love, it's late: let's stay."

Then slow I set myself to count
the strong surges of sea water
the air bore up into my eyes
from the mass of the tall schooner.

Sulle rive del Lambro

Illeso sparí da noi quel giorno
nell'acqua coi velieri capovolti.
Ci lasciarono i pini,
parvenza di fumo sulle case,
e la marina in festa
con voce alle bandiere
di piccoli cavalli.

Nel sereno colore
che qui risale a morte della luna
e affila i colli di Brianza,
tu ancora vaga movendo
hai pause di foglia.

Le api secche di miele
leggere salgono con le spoglie dei grani,
già mutano luce le Vergilie.

Al fiume che solleva ora in un tonfo
di ruota il vuoto della valle,
si rinnova l'infanzia giocata coi sessi.

Mi abbandono al suo sangue
lucente sulla fronte,
alla sua voce in servitú di dolore
funesta nel silenzio del petto.
Tutto che mi resta è già perduto:

On the Banks of the Lambro

Intact, that day vanished from us
in the water with tumbled sails.
The pines deserted us, the semblance
of smoke above the houses
and the waterfront on holiday
with flags that fluttering neighed
like foals.

In the serene tone
that rises here at death of moon
and whets Brianza's hills, you still
moving longingly
have leaf-like pause.

The bees dried of honey
lightly climb with spoils of grain,
the Pleiades already change their light.

At the river that now, with a wheel's
splash, stirs up the hollow of the valley,
childhood, with the sexes played, renews.

I yield to its blood
bright on the brow,
to its voice in servitude of sorrow
mournful in the silence of the breast.
All that is left me is already lost.

Nel nord della mia isola e nell'est
è un vento portato dalle pietre
ad acque amate: a primavera
apre le tombe degli Svevi;
i re d'oro si vestono di fiori.

Apparenza d'eterno alla pietà
un ordine perdura nelle cose
che ricorda l'esilio:
Sul ciglio della frana
èsita il macigno per sempre,
la radice resiste ai denti della talpa.
E dentro la mia sera uccelli
odorosi di arancia oscillano
sugli eucalyptus.

Qui autunno è ancora nel midollo
delle piante; ma covano i sassi
nell'alvo di terra che li tiene;
e lunghi fiori bucano le siepi.
Non ricorda ribrezzo ora il tepore
quasi umano di corolle pelose.

Tu in ascolto sorridi alla tua mente:
E quale sole lèviga i capelli
a fanciulle in corsa;
che gioie mansuete e confuse paure
e gentilezza di pianto lottato,
risorgono nel tempo che s'uguaglia!
Ma come autunno, nascosta è la tua vita.

North and east upon my island
is a wind borne from beloved
stones and waters: in the spring
it opens the tombs of the Suabians;
the kings of gold attire themselves with flowers.

Semblance of eternity for piety,
in things endures an order
that recalls the exile:
On the rim of the avalanche
the rock forever hesitates,
the root resists the teeth of the mole.
And within my evening, birds
odorous of orange sway
on the eucalyptus trees.

Here autumn still is in the pith
of plants; but in the womb of earth
that holds them, brood the stones;
and long flowers pierce the hedges.
Remember not with loathing now the almost
human warmth of hairy corollas.

You, listening, smile in revery:
And what sun smooths the hairs
of young girls, racing;
what mild joys and dark fears
and gentleness of striven tears,
resurge within the time that levels!
But like autumn, your life is concealed.

Anche tramonta questa notte
nei pozzi dei declivi; e rulla il secchio
verso il cerchio dell'alba.
Gli alberi tornano di là dai vetri
come navi fiorite.
                O cara,
come remota, morte era da terra.

This night, too, sets
in the wells of the slopes; the bucket rolls
towards the circle of the dawn.
The trees beyond the windows like
flowered ships return.
O love,
how distant, dead it was from earth.

Elegos per la danzatrice Cumani

Il vento delle selve
chiaro corre alle colline.
Precoce aggiorna: l'adolescente,
del sangue, ha simile sgomento.

E l'orma dell'acqua è l'alba
sulla riva. Si esauriva in me
il supplizio della sabbia,
a batticuore, spaziando la notte.

Duole durevole antichissimo grido:
pietà per l'animale giovane
colpito a morte fra l'erbe
d'agro mattino dopo le piogge nuove.

La terra è in quel petto disperato,
e ivi ha misura la mia voce:

Tu danzi al suo numero chiuso
e torna il tempo in fresche figure:
anche dolore, ma cosí a quiete
vòlto che per dolcezza arde.

In questo silenzio che ràpido consuma
non mi travolgere effimero,
non lasciarmi solo alla luce;

ora che in me a mite fuoco,
nasci Anadiomene.

Elegos for the Dancer Cumani

The wind of the woods
races brightly to the hills.
Precociously day breaks: just as the blood
dismays the adolescent.

And the water's track is dawn
upon the shore. In me exhausted was
the torment of the sand,
to heart-beats, roving the night.

The durable most ancient cry pains:
pity for the youthful animal
struck dead among the grasses
of bitter morning after the new rains.

The earth is in that desperate breast,
and there my voice has measure:

You dance to its closed number
and time returns in fresh figures:
sadness too, but so to quiet
turned, that through sweetness it burns.

In this silence swiftly consuming
confound me not ephemeral,
leave me not alone in light;

now that in mild fire in me,
you are born Anadyomene.

Delfica

Nell'aria dei cedri lunari,
al segno d'oro udimmo il Leone.
Presagio fu l'ululo terreno,
Svelata è la vena di corolla
sulla tempia che declina al sonno
e la tua voce orfica e marina.

Come il sale dall'acque
io esco dal mio cuore.
Dilegua l'età dell'alloro
e l'inquieto ardore
e la sua pietà senza giustizia.

Perisce esigua
l'invenzione dei sogni
alla tua spalla nuda
che di miele odora.

In te salgo, o delfica,
non piú umano. Segreta
la notte delle piogge di calde lune

ti dorme negli occhi:
a questa quiete di cieli in rovina
accade l'infanzia inesistente.

Nei moti delle solitudini stellate,
al rompere dei grani,
alla volontà delle foglie,
sarai urlo della mia sostanza.

Delphic Woman

In the air of lunar cedars,
at the sign of gold we heard the Lion.
The earthly wail foretold.
Unveiled is the vein of corolla
on the temple that slopes to sleep
and your voice orphic and marine.

As salt from water
I issue from my heart.
The age of laurel vanishes
and the unquiet ardour
and its pity without justice.

At your naked shoulder
odorous of honey
perishes exiguous
the invention of dreams.

In you I rise, o Delphic woman,
no longer human. Secret
the night of the warm moons' rains

sleeps in your eyes:
to this quiet of skies in ruins
occurs the inexistent childhood.

In the movements of starred solitudes,
to the bursting of the grains,
to the will of the leaves,
you will be howl of my substance.

Cavalli di luna e di vulcani

ALLA FIGLIA

Isole che ho abitato
verdi su mari immobili.

D'alghe arse, di fossili marini
le spiagge ove corrono in amore
cavalli di luna e di vulcani.

Nel tempo delle frane,
le foglie, le gru assalgono l'aria:
in lume d'alluvione splendono
cieli densi aperti agli stellati;

le colombe volano
dalle spalle nude dei fanciulli.

Qui finita è la terra:
con fatica e con sangue
mi faccio una prigione.

Per te dovrò gettarmi
ai piedi dei potenti,
addolcire il mio cuore di predone.

Ma cacciato dagli uomini,
nel fulmine di luce ancora giaccio
infante a mani aperte,
a rive d'alberi e fiumi:

ivi la latomía l'arancio greco
feconda per gl'imenei dei numi.

Horses of Moon and of Volcanoes

TO MY DAUGHTER

Islands I have dwelt in,
green on immobile seas;

of burnt seaweed, of sea fossils
the beaches where run in heat
horses of moon and of volcanoes.

In the landslide season,
the leaves, the cranes assail the air;
in the light of alluvion, gleam
skies dense and open to the stars;

the doves fly
from the naked shoulders of children.

Here the earth is done:
with toil and blood
I make for me a prison.

For you shall I have to cast me down
at the feet of the mighty,
make soft my plundering heart.

But driven-off by men, again
I lay me down in the flash of light,
a child with open hands
on the banks of trees and rivers:

there, for matings of the gods, the quarry
fruitful makes the grecian orange tree.

Ancora un verde fiume

Ancora un verde fiume mi rapina
e concordia d'erbe e pioppi,
ove s'oblia lume di neve morta.

E qui nella notte, dolce agnello
ha urlato con la testa di sangue:

diluvia in quel grido il tempo
dei lunghi lupi invernali,
del pozzo patria del tuono.

Again a Green River

Again a green river plunders me
and accord of grass and poplars,
where the gleam of dead snow is forgotten.

And here within the night, mild lamb
has howled with head of blood:

there floods, in that outcry, the time
of the long wolves of winter,
of the well, homeland of thunder.

Già vola il fiore magro

Non saprò nulla della mia vita,
oscuro monotono sangue.

Non saprò chi amavo, chi amo,
ora che qui stretto, ridotto alle mie membra,
nel guasto vento di marzo
enumero i mali dei giorni decifrati.

Già vola il fiore magro
dai rami. E io attendo
la pazienza del suo volo irrevocabile.

The Scrawny Flower Already Flies

I shall know nothing of my life,
obscure monotonous blood.

I shall not know whom I have loved, whom I do love
now that here—straitened, lessened to my limbs—
in the wasted wind of March
I enumerate the evils of deciphered days.

The scrawny flower already flies
from the branches. And I wait
the patience of its irrevocable flight.

Davanti al simulacro d'Ilaria del Carretto

Sotto tenera luna già i tuoi colli,
lungo il Serchio fanciulle in vesti rosse
e turchine si muovono leggere.
Cosí al tuo dolce tempo, cara; e Sirio
perde colore, e ogni ora s'allontana,
e il gabbiano s'infuria sulle spiagge
derelitte. Gli amanti vanno lieti
nell'aria di settembre, i loro gesti
accompagnano ombre di parole
che conosci. Non hanno pietà; e tu
tenuta dalla terra, che lamenti?
Sei qui rimasta sola. Il mio sussulto
forse è il tuo, uguale d'ira e di spavento.
Remoti i morti e piú ancora i vivi,
i miei compagni vili e taciturni.

Before the Statue of Ilaria Del Carretto

Now your hills beneath a tender moon,
along the Serchio young girls
in red and turquoise dresses lightly move.
Thus, gentle one, in your sweet time;
and Sirius grows dim, each hour grows
more distant, and the seagull rages
on the derelict beaches. The lovers walk
lighthearted in the air of September, their gestures
accompany the shades of words
you recognize. They have no pity; and you,
held fast by earth, o what do you lament?
Here you remain alone. My shuddering
is yours perhaps: mine, too, with wrath and terror.
Remote the dead and even more the living,
my comrades vile and taciturn.

Ora che sale il giorno

Finita è la notte e la luna
si scioglie lenta nel sereno,
tramonta nei canali.

È cosí vivo settembre in questa terra
di pianura, i prati sono verdi
come nelle valli del sud a primavera.
Ho lasciato i compagni,
ho nascosto il cuore dentro le vecchie mura,
per restare solo a ricordarti.

Come sei piú lontana della luna,
ora che sale il giorno
e sulle pietre batte il piede dei cavalli!

Now Day Breaks

The night is done, the moon
slowly melts in the serene,
sets in the canals.

September lives so in this land
of plains, the meadows are as green
as in the valleys of the south in spring.
I have left my comrades,
have hid my heart within the old walls,
to rest alone remembering you.
How you are more distant than the moon,
now day breaks
and on the stones the hoofs of horses beat!

Una sera, la neve

Di te lontana dietro una porta
chiusa, odo ancora il pianto d'animale:
cosí negli alti paesi al vento della neve
ulula l'aria fra i chiusi dei pastori.

Breve gioco avverso alla memoria:
la neve è qui discesa e rode
i tetti, gonfia gli archi del vecchio Lazzaretto,
e l'Orsa precipita rossa fra le nebbie.

Dove l'anca colore dei miei fiumi,
la fronte della luna dentro l'estate
densa di vespe assassinate? Resta il lutto
della tua voce umiliata nel buio delle spalle
che lamenta la mia assenza.

An Evening, the Snow

Again I hear the animal moan
of distant you behind a closed door:
thus, in the highland villages at the wind of snow,
the air that wails among the shepherds' folds.

Brief game that jars the memory:
the snow has fallen here and gnaws
the rooftops, swells the arches of old Lazzaretto,
and the Great Bear plummets red among the mists.

Where is the coloured thigh of my rivers,
the brow of the moon within the summer
thick with assassinated wasps? There rests—the mourning
of your humbled voice in the darkness of shoulders
that lament my absence.

Che vuoi, pastore d'aria?

Ed è ancora il richiamo dell'antico
corno dei pastori, aspro sui fossati
bianchi di scorze di serpenti. Forse
dà fiato dai pianori d'Acquaviva,
dove il Plàtani rotola conchiglie
sotto l'acqua fra i piedi dei fanciulli
di pelle uliva. O da che terra il soffio
di vento prigioniero, rompe e fa eco
nella luce che già crolla; che vuoi,
pastore d'aria? Forse chiami i morti.
Tu con me non odi, confusa al mare
dal riverbero, attenta al grido basso
dei pescatori che alzano le reti.

What Seek You, Shepherd of the Air

And again the call of the ancient
shepherd's horn, harsh on the torrents
white with the sloughs of snakes. Perhaps
it sweeps from the plateaus of Acquaviva,
where the river Plàtani rolls shells
underwater among the feet of olive-skinned
children. O from what land does the gust
of the prisoner wind erupt and echo
in the light that crumbles now: what seek you,
shepherd of the air? Perhaps you call the dead.
You, love, beside me, do not hear—confused
by the sounding sea, attentive to the low cry
of fishermen hauling in their nets.

Imitazione della gioia

Dove gli alberi ancora
abbandonata piú fanno la sera,
come indolente
è svanito l'ultimo tuo passo,
che appare appena il fiore
sui tigli e insiste alla sua sorte.

Una ragione cerchi agli affetti,
provi il silenzio nella tua vita.
Altra ventura a me rivela
il tempo specchiato. Addolora
come la morte, bellezza ormai
in altri volti fulminea.
Perduto ho ogni cosa innocente,
anche in questa voce, superstite
a imitare la gioia.

Imitation of Joy

Where the trees make evening
even more abandoned,
how languidly
your final step has vanished,
like the flower that scarce appears
on the linden, insistent on its fate.

You seek a motive for the feelings,
experience silence in your life.
Mirrored time reveals to me
a different destiny. Beauty flashing
now in other faces, saddens me
like death.
I have lost every innocent thing,
even in this voice, surviving
to imitate joy.

Inizio di pubertà

Saccheggiatrice d'inerzie e dolori,
notte; difesa ai silenzi,
l'età rigèrmina
delle oblique tristezze.

E vedo in me fanciulli
leggiadri ancora sull'anca,
al declivio delle conchiglie
turbarsi alla mia voce mutata.

Verge of Puberty

Pillager of pains and of inertias,
night; a shield for silences,
the age of sadnesses
oblique, regerminates.

And I see young boys in me,
still graceful on the hip,
at the slope of conch shells,
uneasy at my altered voice.

ERATO AND APOLLYON

[1932–1936]

Canto di Apòllion

Terrena notte, al tuo esiguo fuoco
mi piacqui talvolta,
e scesi fra i mortali.

E vidi l'uomo
chino sul grembo dell'amata
ascoltarsi nascere,
e mutarsi consegnato alla terra,
le mani congiunte,
gli occhi arsi e la mente.

Amavo. Fredde erano le mani
della creatura notturna:
alti terrori accoglieva nel vasto letto
ove nell'alba udii destarmi
da battito di colombe.

Poi il cielo portò foglie
sul suo corpo immoto:
salirono cupe le acque nei mari.

Mio amore, io qui mi dolgo
senza morte, solo.

Song of Apollyon

Earthly night, at your meager fire
I was pleased in me at times
and descended among the mortals.

And I saw man
bent over the breast of the beloved
listening to his being born,
and—altered—to the earth consigned,
his hands clasped,
his eyes scorched and his mind.

I loved. Cold were the hands
of the nocturnal creature:
she ingathered steep terrors in that vast bed
where at dawn I heard me wakened
by the beat of doves.

Then the sky bore leaves
on her still body:
sombre rose the waters in the seas.

My beloved, I here grieve
deathless, alone.

Apòllion

I monti a cupo sonno
supini giacciono affranti.

L'ora nasce
della morte piena, Apòllion;
io sono tardo ancora di membra
e il cuore grava smemorato.

Le mie mani ti porgo
dalle piaghe scordate,
amato distruttore.

Apollyon

In sombre sleep, the mountains
lie supine exhausted.

The hour of full
death is born, Apollyon;
my limbs are tardy still; the heart
is heavy, unremembering.

I stretch my hands to you
from forgotten wounds,
beloved destroyer.

L'Ànapo

Alle sponde odo l'acqua colomba,
Ànapo mio; nella memoria geme
al suo cordoglio
uno stormire altissimo.

Sale soavemente a riva,
dopo il gioco coi numi,
un corpo adolescente:

Mutevole ha il volto,
su una tibia al moto della luce
rigonfia un grumo vegetale.

Chino ai profondi lieviti
ripatisce ogni fase,
ha in sé la morte in nuziale germe.

— Che hai tu fatto delle maree del sangue,
Signore? — Ciclo di ritorni
vano sulla sua carne,
la notte e il flutto delle stelle.

Ride umano sterile sostanza.

In fresco oblío disceso
nel buio d'erbe giace:
l'amata è un'ombra e origlia
nella sua costola.

Mansueti animali,
le pupille d'aria,
bevono in sogno.

The Ànapo

On your banks, my Ànapo,
I hear dove water; in memory moans
to its sorrow
loudest rustling.

Rising softly to the shore,
after playing with the gods,
an adolescent body:

Mutable his face,
on a shin bone in the movement of the light
swells a vegetal grume.

Bent over the deep ferments
he re-endures each phase,
bears within him death in nuptial seed.

—Lord, what hast Thou done with the tides
of the blood?—Cycle of returns
vain on his flesh,
night and the surge of the stars.

Sterile substance laughs humanly.

Descended into cool oblivion,
he lies in the dark of grass;
the beloved is a shadow and eavesdrops
in his rib.

Mild animals,
their pupils of air,
they drink in dream.

Al tuo lume naufrago

Nasco al tuo lume naufrago,
sera d'acque limpide.

Di serene foglie
arde l'aria consolata.

Sradicato dai vivi,
cuore provvisorio,
sono limite vano.

Il tuo dono tremendo
di parole, Signore,
sconto assiduamente.

Dèstami dai morti:
ognuno ha preso la sua terra
e la sua donna.

Tu m'hai guardato dentro
nell'oscurità delle viscere:
nessuno ha la mia disperazione
nel suo cuore:

Sono un uomo solo,
un solo inferno.

In Your Light I Shipwreck

I am born in your light I shipwreck,
evening of limpid waters.

The air, consoled,
burns with serene leaves.

Uprooted from the living,
a makeshift heart,
I am vain limit.

For Thy tremendous gift
of words, I pay
assiduously, Lord.

Awake me from the dead:
each one has taken his land,
his woman.

Thou hast seen within me,
in the darkness of my bowels:
no one has found my desperation
in his heart.

I am an only man,
an only hell.

Sovente una riviera

Sovente una riviera
raggia d'astri solenni,
bugni di zolfo sul mio capo
dondolano.

Tempo d'api: e il miele
è nella mia gola
fresca di suono ancora.
Un corvo, di meriggio gira
su arenarie bige.

Arie dilette: cui quiete di sole
insegna morte, e notte
parole di sabbia,

di patria perduta.

Often a Riviera

Often a riviera
gleams with solemn stars,
beehives of sulphur on my head
sway.

Time of bees; and the honey
is in my throat
fresh with sound again;
at noon a raven wanders
on gray sandstones.

Delightful airs: to which the solar quiet
teaches death, and night
words of sand

of homeland—lost.

Isola di Ulisse

Ferma è l'antica voce.
Odo risonanze effimere,
oblío di piena notte
nell'acqua stellata.

Dal fuoco celeste
nasce l'isola di Ulisse.
Fiumi lenti portano alberi e cieli
nel rombo di rive lunari.

Le api, amata, ci recano l'oro:
tempo delle mutazioni, segreto.

Ulysses' Isle

The ancient voice is still.
I hear ephemeral echoes,
oblivion of full night
in the starred water.

Ulysses' isle
is born of the celestial fire.
Slow rivers carry trees and skies
in the roar of lunar shores.

The bees, beloved, bring us gold:
time of the mutations, secret.

Sardegna

Nell'ora mattutina a luna accesa,
appena affiori, geme
l'acqua celeste.

Ad altra foce
piú dolente sostanza
soffiò di vita l'urlo dei gabbiani.

Mi trovo di stessa nascita;
e l'isolano antico,
ecco, ricerca il solo occhio
sulla sua fronte, infulminato,
e il braccio prova
nel lancio delle rupi maestro.

Graniti sfatti dall'aria,
acque che il sonno grave
matura in sale.

La pietà m'ha perduto;
e qui ritrovo il segno
che allo squallido esilio
s'esprime amoroso;
nei nomi di memoria: Siliqua
dai conci di terra cruda,
negli ossami di pietra
in coni tronchi.

Deserto effimero: in cuore gioca
il volume dei colli d'erba giovane;

e la fraterna aura conforta amore.

Sardinia

At daybreak, with the moon alight,
as soon as you emerge, the azure
water moans.

At another rivermouth
more grieving substance
breathed life into the wail of the gulls.

I share your birth;
and, here, the ancient islander
searches for his only eye—
blasted—on his forehead, tries
his masterly arm
in the casting of stones.

Granite rocks undone by the air,
waters that grave slumber
ripens in salt.

Pity has lost me;
and here I find the sign
that speaks with love
to the squalid exile;
in the names of memory: Siliqua
with its slabs of crude earth,
in the bone heaps of stone
in squat cones.

Ephemeral desert: in the heart there plays
the mass of the hills of young grass;

and the fraternal air comforts love.

Airone morto

Nella palude calda confitto al limo,
caro agli insetti, in me dolora
un airone morto.

Io mi divoro in luce e suono;
battuto in echi squallidi
da tempo a tempo geme un soffio
dimenticato.

Pietà, ch'io non sia
senza voci e figure
nella memoria un giorno.

Dead Heron

In the warm swamp, thrust into the slime,
dear to the insects, in me grieves
a dead heron.

I devour me in light and sound;
struck down in squalid echoes,
from time to time a breath, forgotten,
moans.

Mercy, that I not be
without words and forms
one day, in memory.

Latomíe

Sillabe d'ombre e foglie,
sull'erbe abbandonati
si amano i morti.

Odo. Cara la notte ai morti,
a me specchio di sepolcri,
di latomíe di cedri verdissime,

di cave di salgemma,
di fiumi cui il nome greco
è un verso a ridirlo, dolce.

Quarries

Syllables of shadows and leaves,
on the grass, abandonedly
the dead make love.

I hear. Dear is the night to the dead,
for me—a mirror of sepulchers,
of quarries of greenest cedars,

of mines of salt,
of rivers whose Greek names,
spoken, are soft verses.

Insonnia

NECROPOLI DI PANTÀLICA

Un soffio lieto d'alati
a verde lume discorde:
il mare nelle foglie.

Dissòno. E tutto che mi nasce a gioia
dilania il tempo; un'eco appena
ne serba in voce d'alberi.

Amore di me perduto,
memoria non umana:
sui morti splendono stimmate celesti,
gravi stellati scendono nei fiumi:
s'affioca un'ora di pioggia soave,
o muove un canto in questa notte eterna.

Da anni e anni, in cubicolo aperto
dormo della mia terra,
gli òmeri d'alghe contro grige acque:

nell'aria immota tuonano meteore.

Insomnia

NECROPOLIS OF PANTÀLICA

A glad gust of winged things
jarring the green light:
the sea in the leaves.

I am awry. And all that's born in me to joy
time lacerates, leaving only
its faint echo in voice of trees.

My self-love—lost,
memory, not human:
on the dead, celestial stigmata glisten,
grave starshapes fall into the rivers:
An hour grows languid with soft rain
or a song stirs in this eternal night.

Years and years, I sleep
in an open cell of my earth,
seaweed shoulders against gray waters:

in the still air meteors thunder.

Sul colle delle «Terre Bianche»

Dal giorno, superstite
con gli alberi mi umilio.

Assai arida cosa;
a infermo verde amica,
a nubi gelide
rassegnate in piogge.

Il mare empie la notte,
e l'urlo preme maligno
in poca carne affondato.

Un'eco ci consoli della terra
al tardo strazio, amata;

o la quiete geometrica dell'Orsa.

On the Hill of the «Terre Bianche»

Surviving the day
with the trees I humble me.

Enough of arid things:
friends to feeble green,
to chill clouds
resigned in rains.

The night is filled by sea,
and the howl bears down malignly
sunk in little flesh.

An echo of the earth consoles us
at the tardy harrowing, beloved;

or the geometric quiet of the Bear.

Del mio odore di uomo

Negli alberi uccisi
ululano gli inferni:
Dorme l'estate nel vergine miele,
il ramarro nell'infanzia di mostro.

Del mio odore di uomo
grazia all'aria degli angeli,
all'acqua mio cuore celeste
nel fertile buio di cellula.

For My Human Smell

In the murdered trees
infernos wail:
summer slumbers in the virgin honey,
the lizard in its monstrous infancy.

For my human smell
I ask pardon of the air of angels,
of the water—my heart celestial—
in the fertile darkness of the cell.

Nel giusto tempo umano

Giace nel vento di profonda luce,
l'amata del tempo delle colombe.
Di me di acque di foglie,
sola fra i vivi, o diletta,
ragioni; e la nuda notte
la tua voce consola
di lucenti ardori e letizie.

Ci deluse bellezza, e il dileguare
d'ogni forma e memoria,
il labile moto svelato agli affetti
a specchio degli interni fulgori.

Ma dal profondo tuo sangue,
nel giusto tempo umano,
rinasceremo senza dolore.

In the Just Human Time

She lies in the wind of deep light,
beloved of the time of doves.
Alone among the living, choicest one,
you speak of me of waters of leaves;
your voice consoles
the naked night
with gleaming joys and ardours.

Beauty deluded us, the vanishing
of every form and memory.
the fleeting motion unveiled to the feelings
mirroring the inward fires.

But from your deep blood,
in the just human time,
we shall be reborn without sorrow.

Del peccatore di miti

Del peccatore di miti,
ricorda l'innocenza,
o Eterno; e i rapimenti,
e le stimmate funeste.

Ha il tuo segno di bene e di male,
e immagini ove si duole
la patria della terra.

Of the Sinner of Myths

Of the sinner of myths,
recall the innocence,
o Eternal; the ravishments,
and the fatal stigmata.

He bears your sign of good and evil,
and images wherein laments
the fatherland of earth.

SUNKEN OBOE

[1930–1932]

Alla mia terra

Un sole rompe gonfio nel sonno
e urlano alberi;
avventurosa aurora
in cui disancorata navighi,
e le stagioni marine
dolci fermentano rive nascitture.

Io qui infermo mi desto,
d'altra terra amaro
e della pietà mutevole del canto
che amore mi germina
d'uomini e di morte.

Il mio male ha nuovo verde,
ma le mani son d'aria
ai tuoi rami,
a donne che la tristezza
chiuse in abbandono
e mai le tocca il tempo,
che me discorza e imbigia.

In te mi getto: un fresco
di navate posa nel cuore:
passi ignudi d'angeli
vi s'ascoltano, al buio.

To My Earth

A sun bursts swollen into sleep,
and trees howl;
adventurous aurora
where you, unmoored, set sail,
and mild marine seasons
ferment shores that verge on birth.

I here, infirm, awake,
bitter with an other earth
and with the mutable mercy of song
love germinates in me
of men, of death.

My grief bears new green,
but the hands are airy
on your branches,
on women whom sadness
shut in desolation
and time never touches,
that grays me, strips my bark.

In you I cast myself: a coolness
of naves settles in the heart:
naked steps of angels
sound there, in the dark.

Parola

Tu ridi che per sillabe mi scarno
e curvo cieli e colli, azzurra siepe
a me d'intorno, e stormir d'olmi
e voci d'acque trepide;
che giovinezza inganno
con nuvole e colori
che la luce sprofonda.

Ti so. In te tutta smarrita
alza bellezza i seni,
s'incava ai lombi e in soave moto
s'allarga per il pube timoroso,
e ridiscende in armonia di forme
ai piedi belli con dieci conchiglie.

Ma se ti prendo, ecco:
parola tu pure mi sei e tristezza.

Word

You smile that I grow lean for syllables,
bend the hills and heavens, azure hedge
around me, murmuring of elms
and voices of trembling waters;
that I beguile my youth
with clouds and colours
deepened by the light.

I know you. All astray in you
does beauty lift the breasts,
scoop to the loins and in soft motion
widen through the timorous pubes,
then redescend in harmony of forms
to the feet comely with ten conch shells.

But if I take you, lo:
you, too, are word to me and sorrow.

Dormono selve

Matrice secca d'amore e di nati,
ti gemo accanto
da lunghi anni, disabitato.

Dormono selve
di verde serene, di vento,
pianure dove lo zolfo,
era l'estate dei miti,
immobile.

Non eri entrata a vivermi,
presagio di durevole pena:
La terra moriva sulle acque,
antiche mani nei fiumi
coglievano papiri.

Non so odiarti: cosí lieve
il mio cuore d'uragano.

Woods Sleep

Womb dry with loves and births,
long years I moan
uninhabited, beside you.

Asleep—serene
woods of green, of wind,
plains where sulphur
was the summer of myths,
immobile.

You had not come to live upon me,
omen of enduring pain:
The earth was dying on the waters,
ancient hands in rivers
gathered reeds.

I cannot hate you: so light
is my hurricane heart.

Curva minore

Pèrdimi, Signore, ché non oda
gli anni sommersi taciti spogliarmi,
sí che cangi la doglia in moto aperto:
curva minore
del vivere m'avanza.

E fammi vento che naviga felice,
o seme d'orzo o lebbra
che sé esprima in pieno divenire.

E sia facile amarti
in erba che accima alla luce,
in piaga che buca la carne.

Io tento una vita:
ognuno si scalza e vacilla
in ricerca.

Ancora mi lasci: sono solo
nell'ombra che in sera si spande,
né valico s'apre al dolce
sfociare del sangue.

Minor Curve

Lose me, Lord, that I not hear
the silent sunken years despoil me,
that pain to open motion alter:
living's minor
curve is left me.

And make me wind that sails joyous,
or barley seed or seed of leper
that utters itself in full becoming.

And be it easy to love Thee
in grass that strives to light
in wound that pierces flesh.

I try a life:
everyman walks unshod and wavers
in search.

Again you leave me: I am alone
in the shade that spreads into evening,
nor does passage open for
soft outpouring of the blood.

Metamorfosi nell'urna del Santo

I morti maturano,
il mio cuore con essi.
Pietà di sé
nell'ultimo umore ha la terra.

Muove nei vetri dell'urna
una luce d'alberi lacustri:
Mi devasta oscura mutazione,
santo ignoto: gemono al seme sparso
larve verdi:
il mio volto è loro primavera.

Nasce una memoria di buio
in fondo a pozzi murati,
un'eco di timpani sepolti:

sono la tua reliquia
patita.

Metamorphoses in the Urn of the Saint

The dead mature;
with them, my heart.
Self-pity
is earth's final humor.

Stirring in the glass of the urn,
a light of lacustrine trees:
Dark mutation devastates me,
unknown saint: in the scattered seed moan
green maggots:
my visage is their springtime.

A memory of darkness
is born at the bottom of walled-in wells,
an echo of buried drums.

I am your suffered
relic.

La mia giornata paziente

La mia giornata paziente
a te consegno, Signore,
non sanata infermità,
i ginocchi spaccati dalla noia.

M'abbandono, m'abbandono;
ululo di primavera,
è una foresta
nata nei miei occhi di terra.

My Patient Day

My patient day
to Thee, Lord, I consign,
my not cured infirmity,
my knees cleft by boredom.

I abandon me, I abandon me:
wail of springtime
is a forest
born within my eyes of earth.

Dove morti stanno ad occhi aperti

Seguiremo case silenziose,
dove morti stanno ad occhi aperti
e bambini già adulti
nel riso che li attrista,
e fronde battono a vetri tàciti
a mezzo delle notti.

Avremo voci di morti anche noi,
se pure fummo vivi talvolta
o il cuore delle selve e la montagna,
che ci sospinse ai fiumi,
non ci volle altro che sogni.

Where the Dead Stand Open-Eyed

We shall follow silent houses,
where the dead stand open-eyed
and children, made adult already
in the smile that saddens them,
and branches beat at speechless windows
in the middle of the nights.

We, too, shall have voices of the dead,
if ever we have been alive
or the heart of the woods and the mountains
that drove us to the rivers,
had us be no more than dreams.

Verde deriva

Sera: luce addolorata,
pigre campane affondano.
Non dirmi parole: in me tace
amore di suoni, e l'ora è mia
come nel tempo dei colloqui
con l'aria e con le selve.

Sopori scendevano dai cieli
dentro acque lunari,
case dormivano sonno di montagne,
o angeli fermava la neve sugli ontani,
e stelle ai vetri
velati come carte d'aquiloni.

Verde deriva d'isole,
approdi di velieri,
la ciurma che seguiva mari e nuvole
in cantilena di remi e di cordami
mi lasciava la preda:
nuda e bianca, che a toccarla
si udivano in segreto
le voci dei fiumi e delle rocce.

Poi le terre posavano
su fondali d'acquario,
e ansia di noia e vita d'altri moti
cadeva in assorti firmamenti.

Averti è sgomento
che sazia d'ogni pianto,
dolcezze che l'isole richiami.

Green Drift

Evening: grieving light,
lazy bells founder.
Tell me no words: in me is still
the love of sounds, and mine the hour
as in the time of colloquies
with the air and with the woods.

Slumbers descended from the skies
into lunar waters,
houses slept the sleep of mountains,
or the snow stopped angels on the alder trees
and stars at windows
veiled like paper kites.

Green drift of islands,
landfalls of schooners,
the crew that followed seas and clouds
in the chant of oars and cordage
left me the prey:
white and naked, and to touch her
secret sounded
voices of the rocks and rivers.

Then the lands did rest
on acquamarine depths:
uneasy weariness and life of other movements
fell in engulfed firmaments.

To have you is dismay
that repays for all laments,
softness that recalls the islands.

Primo giorno

Una pace d'acque distese,
mi desta nel cuore
d'antichi uragani,
piccolo mostro turbato.

Son lievi al mio buio
le stelle crollate con me
in sterili globi a due poli,
tra solchi d'aurore veloci:
amore di rupi e di nubi.

È tuo il mio sangue,
Signore: moriamo.

First Day

A peace of outspread waters,
awakens me within the heart
of ancient hurricanes,
small uneasy monster.

Weightless in my darkness are
the stars that crumbled with me
in sterile globes of two poles,
between swift daybreaks' furrows:
love of rocks and clouds.

My blood is Thine,
Lord, let us die.

Seme

Alberi d'ombre,
isole naufragano in vasti acquari,
inferma notte,
sulla terra che nasce:

Un suono d'ali
di nuvola che s'apre
sul mio cuore:

Nessuna cosa muore,
che in me non viva.

Tu mi vedi: cosí lieve son fatto,
cosí dentro alle cose
che cammino coi cieli;

che quando Tu voglia
in seme mi getti
già stanco del peso che dorme.

Seed

Trees of shadows,
islands shipwreck in vast aquaria,
infirm night,
on nascent earth.

A sound of leaves
of cloud that opens
on my heart:

No thing dies
that in me lives not.

You see me: I am wrought so lightly,
made so within things
that I tread with the heavens;

that when Thou willest
Thou mightest hurl me into seed
already weary of the weight that sleeps.

Lamentazione d'un fraticello d'icona

Di assai aridità mi vivo,
mio Dio;
il mio verde squallore!

Romba alta una notte
di caldi insetti;

il cordiglio mi slega
la tunica marcia d'orbace:

Mi cardo la carne
tarlata d'ascaridi:
amore, mio scheletro.

Nascosto, profondo, un cadavere
mastica terra intrisa d'orina:

Mi pento
d'averti donato il mio sangue,
Signore, mio asilo:

misericordia!

Lamentation of a Friar in an Ikon

I live on enough aridity,
my God;
my green squalor!

A night drones loud
with warm insects;

lament unfastens
my rotted tunic of wool:

I card my flesh
gnawed by ascarides:
love, my skeleton.

Deep, concealed, a cadaver
chews earth steeped in urine:

I repent
of having given Thee my blood,
Lord, my refuge:

mercy!

Compagno

Non so che luce mi dèsti:
nuziale ellisse di bianco e di celeste
precipita e in me frana. Tu sei,
beata nascita, a toccarmi
e nei silenzi aduni figure dell'infanzia:
mitissimi occhi di pecora trafitta,
un cane che m'uccisero,
e fu un compagno brutto e aspro
dalle scapole secche.

E quel fanciullo io amavo
sopra gli altri; destro
nel gioco della lippa e delle piastre
e tacito sempre e senza riso.

Si cresceva in vista d'alti cieli
correndo terre e vapori di pianeti:
misteriosi viaggi a lume di lucerna,
e il sonno tardo mi chiudeva assorto
nei canti dei pollai, sereni,
nel primo zoccolar vicino ai forni
delle serve discinte.

M'hai dato pianto
e il nome tuo la luce non mi schiara,
ma quello bianco d'agnello
del cuore che ho sepolto.

Comrade

I know not what light wakened me:
nuptial ellipse of white and azure
plummets, avalanches in me. Blessed birth,
you have come to touch me,
assembling, in the silences, the shapes of childhood:
mildest eyes of an impaled sheep,
a dog of mine they killed,
and he a harsh and ugly comrade
with scrawny shoulder blades.

And the boy I loved
above all others; agile
at tipcat and quoits
and silent always and unsmiling.

We grew in the sight of steep skies
travelling lands and mists of planets:
mysterious trips by lantern light
and late-come sleep enclosed me, absorbed
in the serene songs of the chicken roosts,
in the first clatter of shoes near the ovens—
the ungirdled servant girls.

You have given me lament
yet the light does not reveal your name,
only that white lamb's-name
of the heart that I have buried.

Riposo dell'erba

Deriva di luce; labili vortici,
aeree zone di soli,
risalgono abissi: Apro la zolla
ch'è mia e m'adagio. E dormo:
da secoli l'erba riposa
il suo cuore con me.

Mi desta la morte:
piú uno, piú solo,
battere fondo del vento:
di notte.

Repose of Grass

Drift of light; shifting whirlpools,
airy zones of suns,
abysses rise: I bare the sod
that is mine, recline. And sleep:
for ages, the grass reposes
its heart with me.

Death wakens me:
more one, more only,
beating deep of the wind:
of night.

Alla notte

Dalla tua matrice
io salgo immemore
e piango.

Camminano angeli, muti
con me; non hanno respiro le cose;
in pietra mutata ogni voce,
silenzio di cieli sepolti.

Il primo tuo uomo
non sa, ma dolora.

To the Night

From your womb
unremembering I rise
and weep.

Angels tread, mute
with me; things have no breath;
every voice is turned to stone,
silence of buried skies.

Your first man
knows not, yet grieves.

Senza memoria di morte

Primavera solleva alberi e fiumi;
la voce fonda non odo,
in te perduto, amata.

Senza memoria di morte,
nella carne congiunti,
il rombo d'ultimo giorno
ci desta adolescenti.

Nessuno ci ascolta;
il lieve respiro del sangue!

Fatta ramo
fiorisce sul tuo fianco
la mia mano.

Da piante pietre acque,
nascono gli animali
al soffio dell'aria.

Without Memory of Death

Springtime raises trees and rivers;
lost in you, beloved,
I cannot hear the deep voice.

Without memory of death,
joined in the flesh,
the drone of final day
awakens us, adolescents.

No one listens to us;
the light breath of the blood!

Become a branch,
my hand
flowers on your thigh.

Of plants stones waters,
the animals are born
to the breath of the air.

Òboe sommerso

Avara pena, tarda il tuo dono
in questa mia ora
di sospirati abbandoni.

Un òboe gelido risillaba
gioia di foglie perenni,
non mie, e smemora;

in me si fa sera:
l'acqua tramonta
sulle mie mani erbose.

Ali oscillano in fioco cielo,
làbili: il cuore trasmigra
ed io son gerbido,

e i giorni una maceria.

Sunken Oboe

Miser pain, delay your gift
in this my hour
of longed-for abandons.

Chill, again an oboe utters
joy of everlasting leaves,
not mine, and disremembers;

in me, evening falls:
the water sets
on my grassy hands.

In a dim sky, fleeting
wings sway; the heart migrates
and I am fallow

and the days, rubble.

L'acqua infradicia ghiri

Lucida alba di vetri funerari.
L'acqua infradicia ghiri
nel buio vegetale,
dai grumi dei faggi
filtrando inconsapevole
nei tronchi cavi.

Come i ghiri, il tempo che dilegua:
e brucia il tonfo ultimo,
rapina di dolcezze.

Né in te riparo,
abbandonata al sonno
da fresca gioia:
vanamente rinsanguo fatto sesso.

The Water Decomposes Dormice

Lucid dawn of funereal panes.
The water decomposes dormice
in the vegetal dark,
from the clots of beech trees
filtering unknowing
into the hollow trunks.

Like the dormice, time dissolving:
and the final splash scorches,
pillages with softnesses.

Nor in you is shelter,
you abandoned unto slumber
after fresh joy:
in vain, made sex, I gain new blood.

Nell'antica luce delle maree

Città d'isola
sommersa nel mio cuore,
ecco discendo nell'antica luce
delle maree, presso sepolcri
in riva d'acque
che una letizia scioglie
d'alberi sognati.

Mi chiamo: si specchia
un suono in amorosa eco,
e il segreto n'è dolce, il trasalire
in ampie frane d'aria.

Una stanchezza s'abbandona
in me di precoci rinascite,
la consueta pena d'esser mio
in un'ora di là dal tempo.

E i tuoi morti sento
nei gelosi battiti
di vene vegetali
fatti men fondi:

un respirare assorto di narici.

In the Ancient Light of the Tides

Island city
submerged in my heart,
thus I descend in the ancient light
of the tides, near tombs
on the shore of waters
set loose by a joy
of dreamt-on trees.

I call me: a sound is mirrored
in amorous echo:
soft, its secret startles
in broad avalanches of air.

In me there yields a weariness
of precocious rebirths:
the usual pain of being mine
in an hour beyond time.

And I hear your dead
in the jealous throbs
of vegetal veins
made less deep:

an intent breathing of nostrils.

Di fresca donna riversa in mezzo ai fiori

S'indovinava la stagione occulta
dall'ansia delle piogge notturne,
dal variar nei cieli delle nuvole,
ondose lievi culle;
ed ero morto.

Una città a mezz'aria sospesa
m'era ultimo esilio,
e mi chiamavano intorno
le soavi donne d'un tempo,
e la madre, fatta nuova dagli anni,
la dolce mano scegliendo dalle rose
con le piú bianche mi cingeva il capo.

Fuori era notte
e gli astri seguivano precisi
ignoti cammini in curve d'oro
e le cose fatte fuggitive
mi traevano in angoli segreti
per dirmi di giardini spalancati
e del senso di vita;
ma a me doleva ultimo sorriso

di fresca donna riversa in mezzo ai fiori.

Of Young Woman Bent Back Among the Flowers

One divined the occult season
from the anxiousness of nightly rains,
from clouds that varied in the skies,
wavy light cradles:
and I was dead.

A city hanging in mid-air
was my final exile,
around me called
the soft women of ago,
and, by years renewed, my mother
her gentle hand choosing roses,
with the whitest ones she garlanded my head.

Night outside,
in curves of gold, the stars pursued
precise and unknown paths
and things, made fugitive,
drew me to secret corners
to tell of gardens opened wide
and of the sense of life;
but I was grieved with the final smile

of young woman bent back among the flowers.

Isola

IO NON HO CHE TE,
CUORE DELLA MIA RAZZA.

Di te amore m'attrista,
mia terra, se oscuri profumi
perde la sera d'aranci,
o d'oleandri, sereno,
cammina con rose il torrente
che quasi n'è tocca la foce.

Ma se torno a tue rive
e dolce voce al canto
chiama da strada timorosa
non so se infanzia o amore,
desío d'altri cieli mi volge,
e mi nascondo nelle perdute cose.

Island

I HAVE ONLY YOU,
HEART OF MY RACE.

Love of you saddens me,
my earth, if evening sheds
dark perfumes of orange trees,
or oleanders, if—serene—
the torrent flows with roses
that almost reach its estuary.

But if I return to your shores
and, in song, a soft voice calls,
fearful, from the road—
I know not whether childhood or love,
longing for other skies turns me,
and I hide in the forgotten things.

Preghiera alla pioggia

Odore buono del cielo
sull'erbe,
pioggia di prima sera.

Nuda voce, t'ascolto:
e ne ha primizie dolci di suono
e di rifugio il cuore arato;
e mi sollevi muto adolescente,
d'altra vita sorpreso e d'ogni moto
di súbite resurrezioni
che il buio esprime e trasfigura.

Pietà del tempo celeste,
della sua luce
d'acque sospese;

del nostro cuore
delle vene aperte
sulla terra.

Prayer to the Rain

Fine odour of sky
on green,
rain of early evening.

Nude voice, I listen to you:
in you, the furrowed heart has sweet
first fruits of sound and refuge;
and you awaken me, mute adolescent,
surprised by other life and every motion
by sudden resurrections
that darkness utters and transfigures.

Piety of the celestial time,
of its light
of suspended waters;

of our heart
of veins that open
on the earth.

Amen per la Domenica in Albis

Non m'hai tradito, Signore:
d'ogni dolore
son fatto primo nato.

Amen for the Sunday in Albis

Thou hast not betrayed me, Lord:
of every grief
was I brought forth first-born.

The opening words of the introit for the Sunday in Albis, the first Sunday after Easter, are *Quasi modo*: "*Quasi modo geniti infantes . . .*" ("As newborn babes . . ."), I Pet. 2, 2.

WATERS AND LANDS

[1920–1929]

Ed è subito sera

Ognuno sta solo sul cuor della terra
trafitto da un raggio di sole:
ed è subito sera.

And Suddenly It's Evening

Each alone on the heart of the earth,
impaled upon a ray of sun:
and suddenly it's evening.

Vento a Tíndari

Tíndari, mite ti so
fra larghi colli pensile sull'acque
dell'isole dolci del dio,
oggi m'assali
e ti chini in cuore.

Salgo vertici aerei precipizi,
assorto al vento dei pini,
e la brigata che lieve m'accompagna
s'allontana nell'aria,
onda di suoni e amore,
e tu mi prendi
da cui male mi trassi
e paure d'ombre e di silenzi,
rifugi di dolcezze un tempo assidue
e morte d'anima.

A te ignota è la terra
ove ogni giorno affondo
e segrete sillabe nutro:
altra luce ti sfoglia sopra i vetri
nella veste notturna,
e gioia non mia riposa
sul tuo grembo.

Aspro è l'esilio,
e la ricerca che chiudevo in te
d'armonia oggi si muta
in ansia precoce di morire;

Wind at Tindari

Tindari, I know you mild
among broad hills, above the waters
of the god's soft islands,
today you assail me
and bend into my heart.

I climb peaks, airy precipices,
engulfed in the wind of the pines,
and my lighthearted company
moves far-off in air,
wave of sounds and love,
and you, beloved, take me,
you from whom I drew evil
and fears of shades and silences,
asylums of softness once assiduous
and death of soul.

To you unknown's the earth
wherein each day I sink
and nourish secret syllables:
other light unleafs you through your windows
in your nocturnal dress,
and joy not mine reposes
on your breast.

Harsh is exile,
and my search for harmony
that was to end in you, alters today
into precocious dread of death:

e ogni amore è schermo alla tristezza,
tacito passo nel buio
dove mi hai posto
amaro pane a rompere.

Tíndari serena torna;
soave amico mi desta
che mi sporga nel cielo da una rupe
e io fingo timore a chi non sa
che vento profondo m'ha cercato.

and every love is a screen for sadness,
silent tread into the darkness
where you have set me
bitter bread to break.

Tindari, serene, return;
soft friend awaken me
that from a stone I thrust me skyward,
feigning fear to who knows not
what deep wind has sought me out.

Acquamorta

Acqua chiusa, sonno delle paludi
che in larghe lamine maceri veleni,
ora bianca ora verde nei baleni,
sei simile al mio cuore.

Il pioppo ingrigia d'intorno ed il leccio;
le foglie e le ghiande si chetano dentro,
e ognuna ha i suoi cerchi d'un unico centro
sfrangiati dal cupo ronzar del libeccio.

Cosí, come su acqua allarga
il ricordo i suoi anelli, mio cuore;
si muove da un punto e poi muore:
cosí t'è sorella acquamorta.

Deadwater

Still water, slumber of the marshes,
that steeps venom in broad patches,
now white now green in lightning flashes,
you are like my heart.

Here, the ilex grays, the poplar;
within, the acorns and the leaves grow still;
and each has its single-centred circles
unravelled by the dark drone of the southwester.

Thus, as memory on water
widening its rings, my heart;
she stirs from one point and then dies:
to you, deadwater, she is sister.

Antico inverno

Desiderio delle tue mani chiare
nella penombra della fiamma:
sapevano di rovere e di rose;
di morte. Antico inverno.

Cercavano il miglio gli uccelli
ed erano subito di neve;
cosí le parole.
Un po' di sole, una raggera d'angelo,
e poi la nebbia; e gli alberi,
e noi fatti d'aria al mattino.

Ancient Winter

Desire for your bright hands
in the penumbra of the flame:
they smelt of oak and roses;
of death. Ancient winter.

The birds were seeking grain
and suddenly were snowed under;
thus—words.
A little sun, an angel's glory,
and then the mist; and the trees
and us, made of air in the morning.

Dolore di cose che ignoro

Fitta di bianche e di nere radici
di lievito odora e lombrichi,
tagliata dall'acque la terra.

Dolore di cose che ignoro
mi nasce: non basta una morte
se ecco piú volte mi pesa
con l'erba, sul cuore, una zolla.

Grief of Things That I Know Not

Thick with white and black roots,
odorous of worms and ferment,
severed by the waters—earth.

Grief of things that I know not
is born in me; one death is not enough
if often on my heart, behold,
a sod lies heavy with the grass.

I morti

Mi parve s'aprissero voci,
che labbra cercassero acque,
che mani s'alzassero a cieli.

Che cieli! Piú bianchi dei morti
che sempre mi destano piano;
i piedi hanno scalzi; non vanno lontano.

Gazzelle alle fonti bevevano,
vento a frugare ginepri
e rami ad alzare le stelle?

The Dead

It seemed to me that voices opened,
lips sought water,
hands were lifted to the skies.

What skies! Whiter than the dead
that ever wake me softly;
their feet unshod; they go not far.

Gazelles were drinking at the springs,
wind to seek out junipers
and branches to lift the stars?

Avidamente allargo la mia mano

In povertà di carne, come sono
eccomi, Padre; polvere di strada
che il vento leva appena in suo perdono.

Ma se scarnire non sapevo un tempo
la voce primitiva ancora rozza,
avidamente allargo la mia mano:
dammi dolore cibo cotidiano.

Avidly I Stretch My Hand

In poverty of flesh, as I am
behold me, Father; dust of streets
the pardoning wind lifts lightly.

Yet if once I could not thin
my voice still crude and primitive,
now avidly I stretch my hand:
give me sorrow daily bread.

Day after day

[1943–1946]

Alle fronde dei salici

E come potevamo noi cantare
con il piede straniero sopra il cuore,
fra i morti abbandonati nelle piazze
sull'erba dura di ghiaccio, al lamento
d'agnello dei fanciulli, all'urlo nero
della madre che andava incontro al figlio
crocifisso sul palo del telegrafo?
Alle fronde dei salici, per voto,
anche le nostre cetre erano appese,
oscillavano lievi al triste vento.

On the Willow Branches

And how could we have sung
with the alien foot upon our heart,
among the dead abandoned in the squares
on the grass hard with ice, to the children's
lamb lament, to the black howl
of the mother gone to meet her son
crucified on the telegraph pole?
On the willow branches, by our vow,
our lyres, too, were hung,
lightly they swayed in the sad wind.

Forse il cuore

Sprofonderà l'odore acre dei tigli
nella notte di pioggia. Sarà vano
il tempo della gioia, la sua furia,
quel suo morso di fulmine che schianta.
Rimane appena aperta l'indolenza,
il ricordo d'un gesto, d'una sillaba,
ma come d'un volo lento d'uccelli
fra vapori di nebbia. E ancora attendi,
non so che cosa, mia sperduta; forse
un'ora che decida, che richiami
il principio o la fine: uguale sorte,
ormai. Qui nero il fumo degli incendi
secca ancora la gola. Se lo puoi,
dimentica quel sapore di zolfo,
e la paura. Le parole ci stancano,
risalgono da un'acqua lapidata;
forse il cuore ci resta, forse il cuore . . .

Perhaps the Heart

The acrid odour of the lindens
will sink within the night of rain.
The time of joy, its fury, will be vain,
its lightning bite that shatters.
There scarce remains the indolence,
the memory of a gesture, of a syllable,
but like a slow flight of birds
in fumes of fog. And still you await,
I know not what, my lost one; perhaps
an hour that decides, that recalls
the end or the beginning; henceforward,
equal fates. Here black the smoke
of fires still dries the throat. O if
you can, forget that taste of sulphur,
and the fear. Words wear us out,
they rise again from a stoned water;
perhaps the heart is left us, perhaps the heart . . .

O miei dolci animali

Ora l'autunno guasta il verde ai colli,
o miei dolci animali. Ancora udremo,
prima di notte, l'ultimo lamento
degli uccelli, il richiamo della grigia
pianura che va incontro a quel rumore
alto di mare. E l'odore di legno
alla pioggia, l'odore delle tane,
com'è vivo qui fra le case,
fra gli uomini, o miei dolci animali.
Questo volto che gira gli occhi lenti,
questa mano che segna il cielo dove
romba un tuono, sono vostri, o miei lupi,
mie volpi bruciate dal sangue.
Ogni mano, ogni volto, sono vostri.
Tu mi dici che tutto è stato vano,
la vita, i giorni corrosi da un'acqua
assidua, mentre sale dai giardini
un canto di fanciulli. Ora lontani,
dunque, da noi? Ma cedono nell'aria
come ombre appena. Questa la tua voce.
Ma forse io so che tutto non è stato.

O My Sweet Animals

Now autumn spoils the green of hills,
o my sweet animals. Again we'll hear,
before night falls, the last lament
of birds, the call of the gray plain
that goes to meet that high sound
of the sea. And the smell of wood
in the rain, the smell of dens,
how it lives here among the houses,
among the men, o my sweet animals.
This face that turns its slow eyes,
this hand that points to the sky
where thunder drones, are yours, my wolves,
o my foxes burnt by blood.
Each hand, each face, is yours.
You, love, tell me all was vain:
life, the days corroded by a water
assiduous, while from the gardens
rises a children's song. Are they distant,
then, from us? But they yield in the air,
barely shadows. This your voice.
But I perhaps do know all has not been.

A me pellegrino

Ecco, ritorno nella quieta piazza:
al tuo balcone solitaria oscilla
la bandiera di festa già trascorsa.
— Riappari — dico. Ma solo l'età
che brama i sortilegi, illuse l'eco
delle cave di pietra abbandonate.
Da quanto non risponde l'invisibile
se chiamo come un tempo nel silenzio!
Non sei piú qui, non piú il tuo saluto
giunge a me pellegrino. Mai due volte
la gioia si rivela. E batte estrema
luce sul pino che ricorda il mare.
E vana, anche l'immagine dell'acque.

La nostra terra è lontana, nel sud,
calda di lacrime e di lutti. Donne,
laggiú, nei neri scialli
parlano a mezza voce della morte,
sugli usci delle case.

To Pilgrim Me

Here, I return to the silent square:
on your balcony sways solitary
the banner of a bygone holiday.
—Appear again—I say. But the echo
from abandoned quarries of rock deceived
only the age that yearns for sorcery.
How long since the invisible—if I
should call, as once, in silence—answers not.
You are here no more, no more your greeting
reaches pilgrim me. Never twice
does joy reveal itself. And light extreme
beats on the pine that recalls the sea.
Vain, too, the image of the waters.

Our land is distant, in the south,
warm with tears and mourning. Women
there, in black shawls,
speak of death in lowered voices
at the portals of the houses.

Uomo del mio tempo

Sei ancora quello della pietra e della fionda,
uomo del mio tempo. Eri nella carlinga,
con le ali maligne, le meridiane di morte,
— t'ho visto — dentro il carro di fuoco, alle forche,
alle ruote di tortura. T'ho visto: eri tu,
con la tua scienza esatta persuasa allo sterminio,
senza amore, senza Cristo. Hai ucciso ancora,
come sempre, come uccisero i padri, come uccisero
gli animali che ti videro per la prima volta.
E questo sangue odora come nel giorno
quando il fratello disse all'altro fratello:
« Andiamo ai campi.» E quell'eco fredda, tenace,
è giunta fino a te, dentro la tua giornata.
Dimenticate, o figli, le nuvole di sangue
salite dalla terra, dimenticate i padri:
le loro tombe affondano nella cenere,
gli uccelli neri, il vento, coprono il loro cuore.

Man of My Time

You are still the one with the stone and the sling,
man of my time. You were in the cockpit,
with the malign wings, the sundials of death,
—I have seen you—in the chariot of fire, at the gallows,
at the wheels of torture. I have seen you: it was you,
with your exact science persuaded to extermination,
without love, without Christ. Again, as always, you
have killed, as did your fathers kill, as did
the animals that saw you for the first time, kill.
And this blood smells as on the day
one brother told the other brother: "Let us
go into the fields." And that echo, chill, tenacious,
has reached down to you, within your day.
Forget, o sons, the clouds of blood
risen from the earth, forget the fathers:
their tombs sink down in ashes,
black birds, the wind, cover their heart.

Lettera

Questo silenzio fermo nelle strade,
questo vento indolente, che ora scivola
basso tra le foglie morte o risale
ai colori delle insegne straniere . . .
forse l'ansia di dirti una parola
prima che si richiuda ancora il cielo
sopra un altro giorno, forse l'inerzia,
il nostro male piú vile . . . La vita
non è in questo tremendo, cupo, battere
del cuore, non è pietà, non è piú
che un gioco del sangue dove la morte
è in fiore. O mia dolce gazzella,
io ti ricordo quel geranio acceso
su un muro crivellato di mitraglia.
O neppure la morte ora consola
piú i vivi, la morte per amore?

Letter

This steady silence in the streets,
this lazy wind, that now slides down
among dead leaves, or climbs again
to the colours of alien ensigns . . .
perhaps the anxiety to tell you a word
before the heavens close again
upon another day, perhaps
our vilest ill, inertia . . . Life
is not in this tremendous, sombre
heartbeat, is not pity, is
no longer but a game of the blood
where death's in flower. O my soft
gazelle, recall that geranium kindled
on a bullet-riddled wall.
Or now does even death no longer
console the living, the death for love?

La muraglia

E già sulla muraglia dello stadio,
tra gli spacchi e i ciuffi d'erba pensile,
le lucertole guizzano fulminee;
e la rana ritorna nelle rogge,
canto fermo alle mie notti lontane
dei paesi. Tu ricordi questo luogo
dove la grande stella salutava
il nostro arrivo d'ombre. O cara, quanto
tempo è sceso con le foglie dei pioppi,
quanto sangue nei fiumi della terra.

The Wall

And on the stadium wall already,
among the clefts and tufts of hanging
grass, the lizards lightning flash;
the frog returns to the canals, a steady
song within my distant village
nights. You do recall that here
the great star greeted our arrival
from the shades. O love, how much
time has fallen with the leaves of the poplars,
how much blood into the rivers of the earth.

Di un altro Lazzaro

Da lontanissimi inverni, percuote
un gong sulfureo il tuono sulle valli
fumanti. E come in quel tempo, si modula
la voce delle selve: « Ante lucem
a somno raptus, ex herba inter homines,
surges ». E si rovescia la tua pietra
dove èsita l'immagine del mondo.

Of Another Lazarus

From remotest winters, a sulphureous
gong that hammers thunder on the smoking
valleys. And as in that time, the voice
of woods is modulated: "Ante lucem
a somno raptus, ex herba inter homines,
surges." And your stone is overturned
where hesitates the image of the world.

Giorno dopo giorno

Giorno dopo giorno: parole maledette e il sangue
e l'oro. Vi riconosco, miei simili, o mostri
della terra. Al vostro morso è caduta la pietà,
e la croce gentile ci ha lasciati.
E piú non posso tornare nel mio eliso.
Alzeremo tombe in riva al mare, sui campi dilaniati,
ma non uno dei sarcofaghi che segnano gli eroi.
Con noi la morte ha piú volte giocato:
s'udiva nell'aria un battere monotono di foglie,
come nella brughiera se al vento di scirocco
la folaga palustre sale sulla nube.

Day After Day

Day after day: accursed words and the blood
and the gold. My similars, I recognize you, monsters
of the earth. At your bite is pity fallen,
and the gentle cross has left us.
I can return no more to my elysium.
We shall raise tombs along the sea, upon the lacerated fields,
but yet not one sarcophagus that marks the heroes.
Death has often played with us:
in the air one heard a monotonous beating of leaves,
as on the heath when, in sirocco,
the marsh hen climbs upon the cloud.

Scritto forse su una tomba

Qui lontani da tutti, il sole batte
sui tuoi capelli e vi riaccende il miele,
e noi vivi ricorda dal suo arbusto
già l'ultima cicala dell'estate,
e la sirena che ulula profonda
l'allarme sulla pianura lombarda.
O voci arse dall'aria, che volete?
Ancora sale la noia dalla terra.

Inscription on a Tomb Perhaps

Here, remote from everyone, the sun
beats down on your hair, rekindling honey there,
and from its shrub, the summer's last cicada
now calls us back—us, the living—
as does the siren wailing deep
alarm upon the plain of Lombardy.
O voices scorched by the air, what do you search?
The weariness still rises from the earth.

Dalla rocca di Bergamo Alta

Hai udito il grido del gallo nell'aria
di là dalle murate, oltre le torri
gelide d'una luce che ignoravi,
grido fulmineo di vita, e stormire
di voci dentro le celle, e il richiamo
d'uccello della ronda avanti l'alba.
E non hai detto parole per te:
eri nel cerchio ormai di breve raggio:
e tacquero l'antilope e l'airone
persi in un soffio di fumo maligno,
talismani d'un mondo appena nato.
E passava la luna di febbraio
aperta sulla terra, ma a te forma
nella memoria, accesa al suo silenzio.
Anche tu fra i cipressi della Rocca
ora vai senza rumore; e qui l'ira
si quieta al verde dei giovani morti,
e la pietà lontana è quasi gioia.

From the Fortress of Upper Bergamo

You have heard the cry of the cock in the air
beyond the ramparts, beyond the towers
chill with a light that you knew not,
lightning cry of life, and murmur
in the cells of voices and
the birdcall of the dawn patrol.
For yourself, you spoke no words:
you were in the narrow circle:
and the antelope and the heron stilled
lost in a gust of malignant smoke,
talismans of a world scarce born.
And the February moon did pass
plain upon the earth, for you
but a remembered form, alight in its silence.
You, too, among the cypresses
now soundless walk; and here the wrath
is stilled in the green of the youthful dead
and the distant pity is almost joy.

Milano, agosto 1943

Invano cerchi tra la polvere,
povera mano, la città è morta.
È morta: s'è udito l'ultimo rombo
sul cuore del Naviglio. E l'usignolo
è caduto dall'antenna, alta sul convento,
dove cantava prima del tramonto.
Non scavate pozzi nei cortili:
i vivi non hanno piú sete.
Non toccate i morti, cosí rossi, cosí gonfi:
lasciateli nella terra delle loro case:
la città è morta, è morta.

Milan, August 1943

In vain you search among the dust,
poor hand, the city is dead.
Is dead: the final drone has sounded
on the heart of the Canal;
and from the aerial, high on the convent,
where he sang before the sunset,
fallen is the nightingale.
Dig no wells in the courtyards,
no longer do the living thirst.
Touch not the dead, so red, so swollen:
leave them in their houses' earth:
the city is dead, is dead.

19 gennaio 1944

Ti leggo dolci versi d'un antico,
e le parole nate fra le vigne,
le tende, in riva ai fiumi delle terre
dell'est, come ora ricadono lugubri
e desolate in questa profondissima
notte di guerra, in cui nessuno corre
il cielo degli angeli di morte,
e s'ode il vento con rombo di crollo
se scuote le lamiere che qui in alto
dividono le logge, e la malinconia
sale dei cani che urlano dagli orti
ai colpi di moschetto delle ronde
per le vie deserte. Qualcuno vive.
Forse qualcuno vive. Ma noi, qui,
chiusi in ascolto dell'antica voce,
cerchiamo un segno che superi la vita,
l'oscuro sortilegio della terra,
dove anche fra le tombe di macerie
l'erba maligna solleva il suo fiore.

January 19, 1944

I read to you an ancient one's soft verses,
and the words that were born among the vineyards,
the tents, on the riverbanks of eastern lands,
how sad and desolate they fall in this
profoundest night of war, where no one
crosses the sky of the angels of death,
and the wind is a ruinous roar when it tosses
the metal sheets that here, on high,
divide the balconies, the melancholy
rises from dogs that howl in the gardens
at the rifle shots of the patrols
on the empty streets. Someone's alive.
Perhaps someone's alive. But we, here,
attentive to the ancient voice,
seek a sign that overarches life
the obscure sorcery of earth,
where even among the rubble tombs
the malign grass raises up its flower.

Il traghetto

Di dove chiami? Fioca questa nebbia
di te risuona. Ancora dalle bàite,
è tempo, i cani avidi si lanciano
verso il fiume sulle peste odorose:
luminosa di sangue all'altra riva
sghignazza la faina. È traghetto
che conosco: là, sull'acqua risalgono
ciottoli neri; e quante barche passano
nella notte con fiaccole di zolfo.
Ora sei veramente già lontana
se la voce ha tono innumerevole
d'eco, e appena ne odo la cadenza.
Ma ti vedo: hai viole fra le mani
conserte, cosí pallide, e lichene
vicino agli occhi. Dunque, tu sei morta.

The Ferry

From where do you call? Your echo's faint
within this fog. Again it's time:
from the huts, the eager dogs
rush to the river, to track the scent:
bright with blood, a polecat sneers
upon the other shore. I know
that ferry: there on the water, black
stones emerge; how many ships
pass in the night with sulphur torches.
Now you are truly distant, if your voice
has the measureless tone of echo
and I can barely hear its cadence.
But I see you: you have violets,
so pale, in your clasped hands, and lichens
near your eyes. Thus, you are dead.

Life is not dream

[1946–1948]

Lamento per il Sud

La luna rossa, il vento, il tuo colore
di donna del Nord, la distesa di neve . . .
Il mio cuore è ormai su queste praterie,
in queste acque annuvolate dalle nebbie.
Ho dimenticato il mare, la grave
conchiglia soffiata dai pastori siciliani,
le cantilene dei carri lungo le strade
dove il carrubo trema nel fumo delle stoppie,
ho dimenticato il passo degli aironi e delle gru
nell'aria dei verdi altipiani
per le terre e i fiumi della Lombardia.
Ma l'uomo grida dovunque la sorte d'una patria.
Piú nessuno mi porterà nel Sud.

Oh, il Sud è stanco di trascinare morti
in riva alle paludi di malaria,
è stanco di solitudine, stanco di catene,
è stanco nella sua bocca
delle bestemmie di tutte le razze
che hanno urlato morte con l'eco dei suoi pozzi,
che hanno bevuto il sangue del suo cuore.
Per questo i suoi fanciulli tornano sui monti,
costringono i cavalli sotto coltri di stelle,
mangiano fiori d'acacia lungo le piste
nuovamente rosse, ancora rosse, ancora rosse.
Piú nessuno mi porterà nel Sud.

E questa sera carica d'inverno
è ancora nostra, e qui ripeto a te
il mio assurdo contrappunto
di dolcezze e di furori,
un lamento d'amore senza amore.

Lament for the South

The reddish moon, the wind, your colour
of a woman of the North, the expanse of snow . . .
My heart is now upon these meadows,
in these waters clouded by the mists.
I have forgotten the sea, the grave
conch shell sounded by sicilian shepherds,
the cantilenas of the carts along the streets,
where the carob tree trembles in the smoke of stubble fields.
I have forgotten the passage of the herons and the cranes
in the air of green plateaus
for the lands and streams of Lombardy.
But man will anywhere cry out a homeland's fate.
No one will take me South again.

Oh, the South is tired of hauling the dead
on the banks of malarial marshes,
is tired of solitudes, of chains,
is tired of the curses,
in its mouth, of all the races
that have howled death within the echo of its wells,
that drank the blood of its heart.
For that, its children return to the mountains,
constrain their horses under starry blankets,
eat acacia flowers along the tracks
newly red, still red, still red.
No one will take me South again.

And this night charged with winter
is still ours, and here do I repeat to you
my absurd counterpoint
of sweetnesses and furors,
a lament of love without love.

Epitaffio per Bice Donetti

Con gli occhi alla pioggia e agli elfi della notte,
è là, nel campo quindici a Musocco,
la donna emiliana da me amata
nel tempo triste della giovinezza.
Da poco fu giocata dalla morte
mentre guardava quieta il vento dell'autunno
scrollare i rami dei platani e le foglie
dalla grigia casa di periferia.
Il suo volto è ancora vivo di sorpresa,
come fu certo nell'infanzia, fulminato
per il mangiatore di fuoco alto sul carro.
O tu che passi, spinto da altri morti,
davanti alla fossa undici sessanta,
fermati un minuto a salutare
quella che non si dolse mai dell'uomo
che qui rimane, odiato, coi suoi versi,
uno come tanti, operaio di sogni.

Epitaph for Bice Donetti

With her eyes on the rain and the elfs of the night,
there—in Field Fifteen at Musocco—
lies the woman of Emilia
whom I loved in youth's sad time.
But a while ago, she was tricked by death
as quietly she watched, from her gray house
on the outskirts, the autumn wind toss
the plane tree's branches and the leaves.
Her face is still quick with surprise,
as surely it was in childhood, astonished
by the fire-eater high on the wagon.
O you who pass, drawn by other dead,
before grave number one-hundred-sixty,
stop a moment to salute her—
she who never grieved over the man
who here remains, hated, with his verses,
one like all others, a workman of dreams.

Dialogo

« At cantu commotae Erebi de sedibus imis
umbrae ibant tenues simulacraque luce carentum. »
Siamo sporchi di guerra e Orfeo brulica
d'insetti, è bucato dai pidocchi,
e tu sei morta. L'inverno, quel peso
di ghiaccio, l'acqua, l'aria di tempesta,
furono con te, e il tuono di eco in eco
nelle tue notti di terra. Ed ora so
che ti dovevo piú forte consenso,
ma il nostro tempo è stato furia e sangue:
altri già affondavano nel fango,
avevano le mani, gli occhi disfatti,
urlavano misericordia e amore.
Ma come è sempre tardi per amare;
perdonami, dunque. Ora grido anch'io
il tuo nome in quest'ora meridiana
pigra d'ali, di corde di cicale
tese dentro le scorze dei cipressi.
Piú non sappiamo dov'è la tua sponda;
c'era un varco segnato dai poeti,
presso fonti che fumano da frane
sull'altipiano. Ma in quel luogo io vidi
da ragazzo arbusti di bacche viola,
cani da gregge e uccelli d'aria cupa
e cavalli, misteriosi animali
che vanno dietro l'uomo a testa alta.
I vivi hanno perduto per sempre
la strada dei morti e stanno in disparte.

Questo silenzio è ora piú tremendo
di quello che divide la tua riva.
« Ombre venivano leggere. » E qui

Dialogue

"At cantu commotae Erebi de sedibus imis
umbrae ibant tenues simulacraque luce carentum."
We are filthy with war and Orpheus swarms
with insects, he is pierced by lice,
and you are dead. The winter, that weight
of ice, the water, the tempest air,
were with you, and the thunder of echo
in echo in your earthly nights.
And now I know I owed you stronger
approbation, but our time
was fury and blood: others were foundering
in the mud, had hands and eyes
undone, were howling for mercy and love.
But as it is always late to love;
forgive me, therefore. Now I, too,
cry out your name in this noon hour
lazy with wings, with cords of cicadas
stretched within the cypress barks.
We know no longer where is your shore:
there was a passage marked by poets,
near springs that smoke with landslides on
the high plateau. But there I saw,
as a boy, shrubs of violet berries,
sheep dogs, sombre birds,
and horses, mysterious animals,
behind the man, their heads held high.
The living have forever lost
the way of the dead, and stand apart.

This silence now is more tremendous
than that which separates your shore.
"Frail shadows came." And here

l'Olona scorre tranquillo, non albero
si muove dal suo pozzo di radici.
O non eri Euridice? Non eri Euridice!
Euridice è viva. Euridice! Euridice!

E tu sporco ancora di guerra, Orfeo,
come il tuo cavallo, senza la sferza,
alza il capo, non trema piú la terra:
urla d'amore, vinci, se vuoi, il mondo.

the Olona flows tranquilly,
no tree moves from its well of roots.
O were you not Eurydice? Were you not Eurydice?
Eurydice lives. Eurydice! Eurydice!

And you, still filthy with war, Orpheus,
like your horse, without the whip,
lift up your head, earth quakes no more.
How with love, win, if you will, the world.

ll. 1–2: "Touched by the song, from the deepest Erebus
frail shadows came and semblances bereft of light."
Virgil, *Georgics*, Bk. IV, 471–472

Colore di pioggia e di ferro

Dicevi: morte, silenzio, solitudine;
come amore, vita. Parole
delle nostre provvisorie immagini.
E il vento s'è levato leggero ogni mattina
e il tempo colore di pioggia e di ferro
è passato sulle pietre,
sul nostro chiuso ronzio di maledetti.
Ancora la verità è lontana.
E dimmi, uomo spaccato sulla croce,
e tu dalle mani grosse di sangue,
come risponderò a quelli che domandano?
Ora, ora: prima che altro silenzio
entri negli occhi, prima che altro vento
salga e altra ruggine fiorisca.

Colours of Rain and Iron

You said: death, silence, solitude,
like love, life. Words
of our makeshift images.
And the wind rose light each morning
and the season coloured with rain and iron
passed over the rocks, over
our mewed-up murmur of the damned.
The truth is distant still.
And tell me, man cleft upon the cross
and you with hands thick with blood,
how shall I answer those that ask?
Now, now: before another wind does rise,
another stillness fill the eyes, before
another rust flourishes.

Quasi un madrigale

Il girasole piega a occidente
e già precipita il giorno nel suo
occhio in rovina e l'aria dell'estate
s'addensa e già curva le foglie e il fumo
dei cantieri. S'allontana con scorrere
secco di nubi e stridere di fulmini
quest'ultimo gioco del cielo. Ancora,
e da anni, cara, ci ferma il mutarsi
degli alberi stretti dentro la cerchia
dei Navigli. Ma è sempre il nostro giorno
e sempre quel sole che se ne va
con il filo del suo raggio affettuoso.

Non ho piú ricordi, non voglio ricordare;
la memoria risale dalla morte,
la vita è senza fine. Ogni giorno
è nostro. Uno si fermerà per sempre,
e tu con me, quando ci sembri tardi.
Qui sull'argine del canale, i piedi
in altalena, come di fanciulli,
guardiamo l'acqua, i primi rami dentro
il suo colore verde che s'oscura.
E l'uomo che in silenzio s'avvicina
non nasconde un coltello fra le mani,
ma un fiore di geranio.

Almost a Madrigal

The sunflower bends to the west, and day
already sets in its ruined eye,
the air of summer thickens, curves
the leaves, the smoke of the factories.
With the clouds' dry flow, the lightning's screech
this last game of the heavens moves
far-off. Again, love, as for years,
we pause at the changes in the trees
crowded in the circle of the canals.
But it is still our day, and still
that sun that takes its leave
with the thread of its affectionate ray.

I've no more memories, I do not want to remember;
memory rises up from death,
life is without end. Each day
is ours. One day will stop forever,
and you with me, when it seems late for us.
Here on the edge of the canal, our feet
swinging back-and-forth like children's,
let us watch the water, the first branches
in its darkening green.
And the man who approaches in silence
hides no knife within his hands,
but a geranium.

Thànatos Athànatos

E dovremo dunque negarti, Dio
dei tumori, Dio del fiore vivo,
e cominciare con un no all'oscura
pietra « io sono », e consentire alla morte
e su ogni tomba scrivere la sola
nostra certezza: « thànatos athànatos »?
Senza un nome che ricordi i sogni
le lacrime i furori di quest'uomo
sconfitto da domande ancora aperte?
Il nostro dialogo muta; diventa
ora possibile l'assurdo. Là
oltre il fumo di nebbia, dentro gli alberi
vigila la potenza delle foglie,
vero è il fiume che preme sulle rive.
La vita non è sogno. Vero l'uomo
e il suo pianto geloso del silenzio.
Dio del silenzio, apri la solitudine.

Thànatos Athànatos

And shall we have to deny thee then,
God of the tumors, God of the living
flower, begin with a no to the obscure
rock "I am," consent to death
and on each tomb inscribe our only
certainty: "thànatos athànatos"?
Without a name to tell the dreams
the tears the furors of this man
defeated by still-open questions.
Our dialogue alters; now the absurd
becomes possible. There, beyond
the smoke of fog, within the trees
the power of the leaves is watchful,
true is the river pressing on the banks.
Life is not dream. True is man
and his jealous plaint of silence.
God of silence, open solitude.

Lettera alla madre

« *Mater dulcissima*, ora scendono le nebbie,
il Naviglio urta confusamente sulle dighe,
gli alberi si gonfiano d'acqua, bruciano di neve;
non sono triste nel Nord: non sono
in pace con me, ma non aspetto
perdono da nessuno, molti mi devono lacrime
da uomo a uomo. So che non stai bene, che vivi
come tutte le madri dei poeti, povera
e giusta nella misura d'amore
per i figli lontani. Oggi sono io
che ti scrivo. » — Finalmente, dirai, due parole
di quel ragazzo che fuggí di notte con un mantello corto
e alcuni versi in tasca. Povero, cosí pronto di cuore,
lo uccideranno un giorno in qualche luogo. —
« Certo, ricordo, fu da quel grigio scalo
di treni lenti che portavano mandorle e arance,
alla foce dell'Imera, il fiume pieno di gazze,
di sale, d'eucalyptus. Ma ora ti ringrazio,
questo voglio, dell'ironia che hai messo
sul mio labbro, mite come la tua.
Quel sorriso m'ha salvato da pianti e da dolori.
E non importa se ora ho qualche lacrima per te,
per tutti quelli che come te aspettano,
e non sanno che cosa. Ah, gentile morte,
non toccare l'orologio in cucina che batte sopra il muro
tutta la mia infanzia è passata sullo smalto
del suo quadrante, su quei fiori dipinti:
non toccare le mani, il cuore dei vecchi.
Ma forse qualcuno risponde? O morte di pietà,
morte di pudore. Addio, cara, addio, mia *dulcissima mater*. »

Letter to My Mother

"*Mater dulcissima*, now the mists descend,
the Naviglio dashes against its dikes,
the trees swell with water, burn with snow;
I am not sad in the North: I am not
at peace with myself, but I expect
pardon from no one, many owe me tears,
as man to man. I know you are not well, that you live
like all the mothers of poets, poor
and just in the measure of their love
for distant sons. Today it is I
who write to you."—At last, you will say, two words
from that boy who fled by night in a short coat,
a few lines in his pocket. Poor, so quick of heart,
one day they'll kill him somewhere.
"Surely, I remember, I left from that gray station
of slow trains that carried almonds and oranges,
at the mouth of the Imera, river full of magpies,
salt, of eucalyptus. But now I thank you—
this I would—for the irony you laid upon
my lips, mild as your own.
That smile has saved me from laments and griefs.
And it matters not if now I've some tears for you,
for all who wait—like you—
and know not what they wait. Ah, gentle death,
don't touch the clock in the kitchen that ticks on the wall;
all my childhood has passed on the enamel
of its face, upon those painted flowers:
don't touch the hands, the heart of the dead.
Perhaps someone will answer? O death of mercy,
death of modesty. Farewell, dear one, farewell, my
dulcissima mater."

The false and true green

[1949—1955]

Le morte chitarre

La mia terra è sui fiumi stretta al mare,
non altro luogo ha voce cosí lenta
dove i miei piedi vagano
tra giunchi pesanti di lumache.
Certo è autunno: nel vento a brani
le morte chitarre sollevano le corde
su la bocca nera e una mano agita le dita
di fuoco.
Nello specchio della luna
si pettinano fanciulle col petto d'arance.

Chi piange? Chi frusta i cavalli nell'aria
rossa? Ci fermeremo a questa riva
lungo le catene d'erba e tu amore
non portarmi davanti a quello specchio
infinito: vi si guardano dentro ragazzi
che cantano e alberi altissimi e acque.
Chi piange? Io no, credimi: sui fiumi
corrono esasperati schiocchi d'una frusta,
i cavalli cupi, i lampi di zolfo.
Io no, la mia razza ha coltelli
che ardono e lune e ferite che bruciano.

The Dead Guitars

My land is on the rivers and thrust against the sea,
no other place has voice so lingering
where my footsteps wander
among the rushes heavy with snails.
Surely it is autumn: in the wind in snatches
the dead guitars pluck the cords
on the black mouth, and a hand stirs the fingers
of fire.
In the mirror of the moon
young girls with breasts of oranges dress their hair.

Who weeps? Who whips the horses in the red
air? We shall stop beside this shore
along the chains of grass and you, beloved,
bring me not before that infinite
mirror: there within behold themselves
boys that sing and steepest trees and waters.
Who weeps? I not, believe me: on the rivers
race exasperated flailed by a lash,
the sombre horses, the lightning flashes of sulphur.
I not, my race has knives
that blaze and moons and wounds that burn.

Il falso e vero verde

Tu non m'aspetti piú col cuore vile
dell'orologio. Non importa se apri
o fissi lo squallore: restano ore
irte, brulle, con battito di foglie
improvvise sui vetri della tua
finestra, alta su due strade di nuvole.
Mi resta la lentezza d'un sorriso,
il cielo buio d'una veste, il velluto
colore ruggine avvolto ai capelli
e sciolto sulle spalle e quel tuo volto
affondato in un'acqua appena mossa.

Colpi di foglie ruvide di giallo,
uccelli di fuliggine. Altre foglie
ora screpolano i rami e già scattano
aggrovigliate: il falso e vero verde
dell'aprile, quel ghigno scatenato
del certo fiorire. E tu non fiorisci,
non metti giorni, né sogni che salgano
dal nostro al di là, non hai piú i tuoi occhi
infantili, non hai piú mani tenere
per cercare il mio viso che mi sfugge?
Resta il pudore di scrivere versi
di diario o di gettare un urlo al vuoto
o nel cuore incredibile che lotta
ancora con il suo tempo scosceso.

The False and True Green

No longer wait for me with the coward heart
of the clock. It matters not if you set free
or fix the squalor: all that's left
are hard and ragged hours, the beat
of leaves upon your windowpanes,
steep above two streets of clouds.
I keep the slowness of a smile,
the dark sky of a dress, the rust-
coloured velvet around your hair
and loose on your shoulders, and your face
sunk in water that hardly stirs.

Strokes of leaves rough with yellow,
birds of soot. Other leaves
now cleave the branches, darting out
entangled: April's false and true
green, that unleashed sneer of certain
flowering. And do you flower not,
put on no days, nor dreams that rise
from our beyond? Where are your childlike
eyes, your tender hands
to seek my face that flees me?
There rests, the shyness of writing diary
verses or casting a howl into the void
or into the incredible heart that still
struggles with its ruined time.

In una città lontana

Non apparve dal cielo, ma sul prato
d'alga pallida del giardino nordico
saltò improvviso un corvo giú da foglie
ripide: non simbolo, nell'estate
curva d'arcobaleni e piogge: un corvo
vero come un acrobata al trapezio
del Tivoli.
Fragile, astuta immagine,
entrata nel giorno che finiva in noi
con giostre e ruote di macchine ad acqua
e strofe di ballate
di marinai e l'urlo del distacco
d'una nave che apriva ali furiose
di schiume o di lacrime delle donne
dei porti.
Batteva l'ora su estrema
riva d'Europa, insistente, smaniosa
d'innocenza.
Era il corvo ancora un segno
felice, uguale ad altri
quando provavo la mia mente in ogni
suo limite e figura e trattenevo
un grido per tentare il mondo
fermo, meravigliato di potere
anch'io gridare. Forse gioco, attesa,
violenza: ma per un po' d'ironia
si perde tutto, e fa paura la luce
piú dell'ombra.

In a Distant City

He didn't emerge from the sky, but on the meadow
of pale seaweed in the northern garden—
a raven sudden sprang from the steep
leaves: not a symbol, in the summer
bent with rainbows and rains: a true raven
like an acrobat on the trapeze
at Tivoli.
Fragile, astute image
entering into the day that ended in us
with carousels and paddle wheels
and strophes of sailors'
ballads and the departing wail
of a steamer opening furious wings
of foam or the tears of harbour
women.
The hour struck on this farthest
shore of Europe, insistent, frenzied
for innocence.
The raven was still a happy
sign, like other signs
when I tried out my mind in its every
limit and form, holding back
an outcry to attempt the still
world, amazed that I, too,
could cry out. Perhaps a game, a waiting,
a violence: but for a touch of irony
one loses all, and there's more to be feared in the light
than the shadow.

Aspettavi una parola
a te ignota o mia? Poi il corvo si volse,
staccò le zampe rapide dall'erba
e sparí nell'aria del tuo occhio verde.

Per un po' d'ironia si perde tutto.

My love, did you await
a word unknown to you or my word? Then the raven
turned, lifted his swift feet from the grass
and vanished in the air of your green eye.

For a touch of irony one loses all.

Che lunga notte

Che lunga notte e luna rosa e verde
al tuo grido tra zagare, se batti
ad una porta come un re di Dio
pungente di rugiade: « Apri, amore, apri! »
Il vento, a corde, dagli Iblei, dai coni
delle Madonie, strappa inni e lamenti
su timpani di grotte antiche come
l'agave e l'occhio del brigante. E l'Orsa
ancora non ti lascia e scrolla i sette
fuochi d'allarme accesi alle colline,
e non ti lascia il rumore dei carri
rossi di saraceni e di crociati,
forse la solitudine, anche il dialogo
con gli animali stellati, il cavallo
e il cane, la rana, le allucinate
chitarre di cicale nella sera.

How Long a Night

How long a night, how pink and green the moon
at your outcry among the orange blossoms,
if you pound at a gate like one of God's kings,
pungent with dew: "Open, beloved, open!"
The chorded wind from the Iblei, from the cones
of the Madonie, wrests hymns and laments
from the drums of grottoes ancient as
the agave and the bandit's eye. And the Great Bear
still won't leave you and shakes its seven
bonfires blazing on the hills,
and these are with you still—the sound of the red
chariots of Saracens and Crusaders,
perhaps the solitude and, too, the dialogue
with the starred animals, the horse
and the dog, the frog, the hallucinating
guitars of crickets in the evening.

Vicino a una torre saracena, per il fratello morto

Io stavo ad una chiara
conchiglia del mio mare
e nel suono lontano udivo cuori
crescere con me, battere
uguale età. Di dèi o di bestie, timidi
o diavoli: favole avverse della
mente. Forse le attente
morse delle tagliole
cupe per volpi lupi
iene, sotto la luna a vela lacera,
scattarono per noi,
cuori di viole delicate, cuori
di fiori irti. O non dovevano crescere
e scendere dal suono: il tuono tetro
su dall'arcobaleno d'aria e pietra,
all'orecchio del mare rombava una
infanzia errata, eredità di sogni
a rovescio, alla terra di misure
astratte, ove ogni cosa
è piú forte dell'uomo.

Near a Saracen Tower, for His Dead Brother

I listened to a glistening
shell of my sea
and in the far-off sound I heard
hearts growing with me, beating
equal time. Of gods and beasts, of timid ones
or demons: contrary fables of the
mind. Perhaps the attentive
bite of the dark
snares for foxes wolves
hyenas, under the moon with tattered sails,
snapped for us,
hearts of delicate violets, hearts
of spiny flowers. O they should not have risen
and fallen with the sound: the sombre thunder
up from the rainbow of air and stone,
into the ear of the sea droned
a mistaken childhood, heritage of
dreams awry, to the earth
of abstract measures, where everything
is stronger than man.

Laude
29 Aprile 1945

FIGLIO

— E perché, madre, sputi su un cadavere
a testa in giú, legato per i piedi
alla trave? E non hai schifo degli altri
che gli pendono a fianco? Ah quella donna,
le sue calze da macabro can-can
e gola e bocca di fiori pestati!
No, madre, fermati: grida alla folla
di andare via. Non è lamento, è ghigno,
è gioia: già s'attaccano i tafani
ai nodi delle vene. Hai sparato
su quel viso, ora: madre, madre, madre!

MADRE

— Sempre abbiamo sputato sui cadaveri,
figlio: appesi alle grate di finestre,
ad albero di nave, inceneriti
per la Croce, sbranati dai mastini
per un po' d'erba al limite dei feudi.
E fosse solitudine o tumulto,
occhio per occhio, dente per dente,
dopo duemila anni di eucaristia,
il nostro cuore ha voluto aperto
l'altro cuore che aveva aperto il tuo,
figlio. T'hanno scavato gli occhi, rotto
le mani per un nome da tradire.
Mostrami gli occhi, dammi qui le mani:
sei morto, figlio! Perché tu sei morto
puoi perdonare: figlio, figlio, figlio!

Laud
April 29, 1945

SON

—And why, mother, do you spit at the cadaver
head down, lashed by his feet to the crossbeam?
And don't the others, hanging there
beside him, disgust you? Ah, that woman,
her macabre can-can stockings,
her throat and mouth of trampled flowers!
No, mother, stop: cry to the crowd
to go away. This is no lament, it is sneer,
it is joy: the horseflies are already fast
at the knots of the veins. You have fired
now at that face: mother, mother, mother!

MOTHER

—We have always spat at the cadavers,
son: hanging at the window grates,
at the mast of the ship, incinerated
for the cross, torn limb from limb
for a little grass at the edge of the estates.
And be it solitude or tumult,
eye for eye, tooth for tooth,
after two thousand years of eucharist,
our heart had wanted to open
that other heart that had opened yours,
my son. They have hollowed your eyes, shattered
your hands for a name to be betrayed.
Show me your eyes; give me here your hands:
son, you are dead! Because you are dead,
you can pardon: son, son, son.

FIGLIO

— Quest'afa ripugnante, questo fumo
di macerie, le grasse mosche verdi
a grappoli agli uncini: l'ira e il sangue
colano giustamente. Non per te
e non per me, madre: occhi e mani ancora
mi bucheranno domani. Da secoli
la pietà è l'urlo dell'assassinato.

SON

—This repugnant sultry heat, this smoke
of rubble, the fat green flies
in clusters on the hooks: the wrath and the blood
flow justly. Not for you
and, mother, not for me: again tomorrow they will
pierce my eyes and hands. For centuries
mercy is the howl of the assassinated.

Auschwitz

Laggiú, ad Auschwitz, lontano dalla Vistola,
amore, lungo la pianura nordica,
in un campo di morte: fredda, funebre,
la pioggia sulla ruggine dei pali
e i grovigli di ferro dei recinti:
e non albero o uccelli nell'aria grigia
o su dal nostro pensiero, ma inerzia
e dolore, che la memoria lascia
al suo silenzio senza ironia o ira.

Tu non vuoi elegie, idilli: solo
ragioni della nostra sorte, qui,
tu, tenera ai contrasti della mente,
incerta a una presenza
chiara della vita. E la vita è qui,
in ogni no che pare una certezza:
qui udremo piangere l'angelo, il mostro,
le nostre ore future
battere l'al di là, che è qui, in eterno
e in movimento, non in un'immagine
di sogni, di possibile pietà.
E qui le metamorfosi, qui i miti.
Senza nome di simboli o d'un dio,
sono cronaca, luoghi della terra,
sono Auschwitz, amore. Come subito
si mutò in fumo d'ombra
il caro corpo d'Alfeo e d'Aretusa!

Da quell'inferno aperto da una scritta
bianca: « Il lavoro vi renderà liberi »
uscí continuo il fumo
di migliaia di donne, spinte fuori

Auschwitz

There, at Auschwitz, distant from the Vistula,
love, along the northern plain,
in a camp of death: funereal, chill,
the rain upon the rusty poles
and the tangled iron of the fences:
and neither tree nor birds in the gray air
or above our revery, but inertia
and pain, that memory bequeaths unto
its silence without irony or ire.

You seek no idylls, elegies: only
motives for our destiny, you tender
here before the contrasts of the mind,
uncertain at a clear
presence that is life's. But life is here,
in every no that seems a certainty:
here we shall hear the angel weep, the monster,
hear our future hours
beating on the beyond, that now is here
in movement and eternity, not in
an image of dreams, of possible piety.
And here the metamorphoses, the myths.
They bear no name of symbols or a god,
are chronicle, are places of the earth,
they are Auschwitz, love. How suddenly
to smoke of shadow altered
dear flesh of Alpheus and Arethusa!

From that inferno opened by a white
inscription: "Labor will make you free"
issued continually
the smoke of thousands of women, from the kennels

all'alba dai canili contro il muro
del tiro a segno o soffocate urlando
misericordia all'acqua con la bocca
di scheletro sotto le docce a gas.
Le troverai tu, soldato, nella tua
storia, in forme di fiumi, d'animali,
o sei tu pure cenere d'Auschwitz,
medaglia di silenzio?
Restano lunghe trecce chiuse in urne
di vetro, ancora strette da amuleti
e ombre infinite di piccole scarpe
e di sciarpe d'ebrei: sono reliquie
d'un tempo di saggezza, di sapienza
dell'uomo che si fa misura d'armi,
sono i miti, le nostre metamorfosi.

Sulle distese, dove amore e pianto
marcirono e pietà, sotto la pioggia,
laggiú, batteva un no dentro di noi,
un no alla morte, morta ad Auschwitz,
per non ripetere, da quella buca
di cenere, la morte.

forward thrust at dawn against the target
wall or suffocated howling mercy
unto water with the skeletal mouth
under the showers of gas.
You will find them, soldier, there within
your history, within the forms of streams,
of animals, or are you, too, but ash
of Auschwitz, medal of silence?
Long braids remain enclosed in urns of glass,
still crowded by amulets and infinite
shades of little shoes and shawls of Jews:
they are relics of a time of wisdom,
of man who makes of arms the measure, they
are the myths, our metamorphoses.

Upon the plains, where love and lamentation
rotted and piety, beneath the rain,
there, a no within us beat, a no
to death, at Auschwitz dead, that from that pit
of ash, death not repeat.

The incomparable earth

[1955–1958]

I say that the dead slay the living

Aeschylus: *Choephoroe*, V. 886

Visibile, invisibile

Visibile, invisibile
il carrettiere all'orizzonte
nelle braccia della strada chiama
risponde alla voce delle isole.
Anch'io non vado alla deriva,
intorno rulla il mondo, leggo
la mia storia come guardia di notte
le ore delle piogge. Il segreto ha margini
felici, stratagemmi, attrazioni difficili.
La mia vita, abitanti crudeli e sorridenti
delle mie vie, dei miei paesaggi,
è senza maniglie alle porte.
Non mi preparo alla morte,
so il principio delle cose,
la fine è una superficie dove viaggia
l'invasore della mia ombra.
Io non conosco le ombre.

Visible, Invisible

Visible, invisible
the waggoner on the horizon
in the arms of the road calls out,
answering the voice of the islands.
I, too, am not adrift,
the world revolves, I read
my history as a night watchman
reads the hours of rain. The secret has happy
margins, stratagems, difficult attractions.
My life—smiling, cruel inhabitants
of my ways, my landscapes—
has no handles at its doors.
I don't prepare myself for death,
I know the origin of things,
the end is a surface on which journeys
the invader of my shadow.
I do not know the shadows.

Da tempo ti devo parole d'amore:
o sono forse quelle che ogni giorno
sfuggono rapide appena percosse
e la memoria le teme, che muta
i segni inevitabili in dialogo
nemico a picco con l'anima. Forse
il tonfo della mente non fa udire
le mie parole d'amore o la paura
dell'eco arbitraria che sfoca
l'immagine piú debole d'un suono
affettuoso: o toccano l'invisibile
ironia, la sua natura di scure
o la mia vita già accerchiata, amore.
O forse è il colore che le abbaglia
se urtano con la luce
del tempo che verrà a te quando il mio
non potrà piú chiamare amore oscuro
amore già piangendo
la bellezza, la rottura impetuosa
con la terra impareggiabile, amore.

The Incomparable Earth

Long since I owe you words of love:
or they're the words, perhaps, that flee
each day when they are barely struck,
words that are feared by memory
that alters the inevitable
signs into hostile dialogue
that sinks with the soul. Perhaps
my words of love are drowned by the thud
of the mind or the fear of the arbitrary
echo from even the frailest image
of a fond sound: or they touch the invisible
irony, that's like an axe,
or—love—my life, by now beleaguered.
Or colour dazzles them, perhaps,
When they clash with the light
of the time that will come to you when my
time can no longer call love dark
love already weeping
the beauty, the impetuous rupture
with the incomparable earth.

Oggi ventuno marzo

Oggi ventuno marzo entra l'Ariete
nell'equinozio e picchia la sua
testa maschia contro alberi e rocce,
e tu amore stacchi
ai suoi colpi il vento d'inverno
dal tuo orecchio inclinato
sull'ultima mia parola. Galleggia
la prima schiuma sulle piante, pallida
quasi verde e non rifiuta
l'avvertimento. E la notizia corre
ai gabbiani che s'incontrano
fra gli arcobaleni: spuntano
scrosciando il loro linguaggio
di spruzzi che rintoccano
nelle grotte. Tu copri il loro grido
al mio fianco, apri il ponte
fra noi e le raffiche
che la natura prepara sottoterra
in un lampo privo di saggezza,
oltrepassi la spinta dei germogli.
Ora la primavera non ci basta.

Today the Twenty-First of March

Today, the twenty-first of March, the Ram
enters the equinox, battering his
male head against the trees and rocks,
and you, love, at his blows, remove
the winter wind from your ear bent down to hear
my latest word. The first froth
floats upon the plants, pale-
almost-green it does not shun
the omen. Tidings run
to the gulls that gather
among the rainbows: they emerge,
their language splashed
with spray that tolls
in the grottoes. At my side,
you drown their outcry, open the bridge
between us and the gusts
that nature, underground, prepares
in a flash that has no wisdom;
you pass beyond the thrust of the buds.
Now spring is not enough for us.

In questa città

In questa città c'è pure la macchina
che stritola i sogni: con un gettone
vivo, un piccolo disco di dolore
sei subito di là, su questa terra,
ignoto in mezzo ad ombre deliranti
su alghe di fosforo funghi di fumo:
una giostra di mostri
che gira su conchiglie
che si spezzano putride sonando.
È in un bar d'angolo laggiú alla svolta
dei platani, qui nella mia metropoli
o altrove. Su, già scatta la manopola.

In This City

This city has even got the machine
that grinds out dreams: with a quick
token, a little disk of pain,
in no time you're off, upon this earth,
unknown in a pack of raving shadows
on phosphorus seaweed, mushrooms of smoke:
a merry-go-round of monsters
revolving on conch shells
that fall to putrid pieces when they play.
It's in a bar down there at the turn
of the plane trees, here in my metropolis
or elsewhere. Come, the switch is on!

Micene

Sulla strada di Micene alberata
di eucalyptus puoi trovare formaggio
di pecora e vino resinato "À la belle
Hélène de Ménélas," un'osteria
che svia il pensiero dal sangue
degli Atridi. La tua reggia, Agamennone,
è covo di briganti sotto il monte
Zara di sasso non scalfito
da radici a strapiombo su burroni
sghembi. I poeti parlano molto
di te, dell'invenzione del delitto
nella tua casa di crisi,
del furore funebre di Elettra,
che nutrí per dieci anni con l'occhio
del sesso il fratello lontano
al matricidio, parlano i diabolici
della logica della regina,
la moglie del soldato assente
Agamennone, mente, spada tradita.
E tu solo ti sei perduto,
Oreste, il tuo viso scomparve senza
maschera d'oro. Ai Leoni della porta,
agli scheletri dell'armonia scenica
rialzati dai filologi delle pietre,
il mio saluto di siculo greco.

Mycenae

On the road that runs through Mycenae, lined
with eucalyptus, you can find
sheep's-milk cheese and scented wine
"A la belle Hélène de Ménélas,"
a tavern that veers the mind from the blood
of the Atreides. Your kingdom, Agamemnon,
is a bandit's den beneath Mount Zara,
jutting over crooked gullies,
its stone not scarred by roots. The poets
speak much of you, of the crime invented
in your house of crisis,
of Electra's funereal frenzy,
that nurtured—with the eye of sex,
for ten long years—her distant brother
to matricide; the diabolical
speak of the logic of the queen,
wife of the absent soldier,
Agamemnon, mind and sword betrayed.
And only you are lost,
Orestes, your visage vanished without
a golden mask. To the Lions at the gate,
to the skeletons of that scenic harmony
philologists have raised up from the stones,
my greeting of a Greek Sicilian.

Alla nuova luna

In principio Dio creò il cielo
e la terra, poi nel suo giorno
esatto mise i luminari in cielo
e al settimo giorno si riposò.

Dopo miliardi di anni l'uomo,
fatto a sua immagine e somiglianza,
senza mai riposare, con la sua
intelligenza laica,
senza timore, nel cielo sereno
d'una notte d'ottobre,
mise altri luminari uguali
a quelli che giravano
dalla creazione del mondo. Amen.

To the New Moon

In the beginning God created the heaven
and the earth, then in His exact
day he set the lights in heaven
and on the seventh day He rested.

After millions of years, man,
made in His image and likeness,
never resting, with his
secular intelligence,
without fear, in the serene sky
of an October night,
set other luminaries like
those that turned
since the creation of the world. Amen.

Una risposta

Se arde alla mente l'àncora d'Ulisse . . .
Se in riva al mare di Aci, qui fra barche
con l'occhio nero a prua contro la mala
sorte, io potessi dal nulla dell'aria
qui dal nulla che stride di colpo e uncina
come la fiocina del pesce-spada,

dal nulla delle mani che si mutano
come Aci, viva formare dal nulla
una formica e spingerla nel cono
di sabbia del suo labirinto o un virus
che dia continua giovinezza al mio
piú fedele nemico,
forse allora sarei simile a Dio —

nell'uguale fermezza della vita
e della morte non contrarie:
onda qui e lava, larve
della luce di questa già futura
chiara mattina d'inverno — risposta
a una domanda di natura e angoscia
che folgora su un numero miliare,
il primo della strada torrida
che s'incunea nell'al di là.

An Answer

If the anchor of Ulysses burns in the mind . . .
If, on the shore of Acis' sea,
among the boats, my black eye set
to the prow against the evil fate,
I could, from the null of the air,
here from the null that sudden shrills
and hooks like the beak of the swordfish,

from the null of the hands that change like Acis,
form out of the null a living
ant and thrust it into the sandy
cone of its labyrinth, or a virus
that would give eternal youth to my
most faithful enemy,
then would I perhaps be like to God—

in equal steadiness of life
and death, not contraries:
wave and lava here, larvae
of light for the already future
glistening winter morning—answer
to a claim of nature, an anguish
that blazes on a milestone number,
the first on the torrid road
that drives like a wedge into the beyond.

Altra risposta

Ma che volete pidocchi di Cristo?
Non accade nulla nel mondo e l'uomo
stringe ancora la pioggia nelle sue ali
di corvo e grida amore e dissonanza.
Per voi non manca sangue
dall'eternità. Soltanto la pecora
si torse al suo ritorno con la testa
brulla e l'occhio di sale.
Ma non accade nulla. E già è muschio
la cronaca ai muri della città
d'un arcipelago lontano.

Other Answer

But what do you want, lice of Christ?
Nothing happens in the world and man
still hugs the rain in his raven wings
and cries out love and dissonance.
Since eternity, you've never
lacked for blood. Only the sheep
turned round on its way back with ragged
head and eyes of salt.
But nothing happens. And moss already—
the chronicle on the walls of the city
of a distant archipelago.

Al padre

Dove sull'acque viola
era Messina, tra fili spezzati
e macerie tu vai lungo binari
e scambi col tuo berretto di gallo
isolano. Il terremoto ribolle
da tre giorni, è dicembre d'uragani
e mare avvelenato. Le nostre notti cadono
nei carri merci e noi bestiame infantile
contiamo sogni polverosi con i morti
sfondati dai ferri, mordendo mandorle
e mele disseccate a ghirlanda. La scienza
del dolore mise verità e lame
nei giochi dei bassopiani di malaria
gialla e terzana gonfia di fango.

La tua pazienza
triste, delicata, ci rubò la paura,
fu lezione di giorni uniti alla morte
tradita, al vilipendio dei ladroni
presi fra i rottami e giustiziati al buio
dalla fucileria degli sbarchi, un conto
di numeri bassi che tornava esatto
concentrico, un bilancio di vita futura.

Il tuo berretto di sole andava su e giú
nel poco spazio che sempre ti hanno dato.
Anche a me misurarono ogni cosa,
e ho portato il tuo nome
un po' piú in là dell'odio e dell'invidia.
Quel rosso sul tuo capo era una mitria,
una corona con le ali d'aquila.
E ora nell'aquila dei tuoi novant'anni

To My Father

Where Messina lay
violet upon the waters, among the mangled wires
and rubble, you walk along the rails
and switches in your islander's
cock-of-the-walk beret. For three days now,
the earthquake boils, it's hurricane December
and a poisoned sea. Our nights fall
into the freight cars; we, young livestock,
count our dusty dreams with the dead
crushed by iron, munching almonds
and apples dried in garlands. The science
of pain put truth and blades into our games
on the lowlands of yellow malaria
and tertian fever swollen with mud.

Your patience, sad and delicate,
robbed us of fear,
a lesson of days linked to the death
we had betrayed, to the scorn of the thieves
seized among the debris, and executed in the dark
by the firing squads of the landing parties, a tally
of low numbers adding up exact
concentric, a scale of future life.

Back and forth your sun cap moved
in the little space they always left you.
For me, too, everything was measured
and I have borne your name
a little beyond the hatred and the envy.
That red on your cap was a mitre,
a crown with eagle's wings.
And now in the eagle of your ninety years

ho voluto parlare con te, coi tuoi segnali
di partenza colorati dalla lanterna
notturna, e qui da una ruota
imperfetta del mondo,
su una piena di muri serrati,
lontano dai gelsomini d'Arabia
dove ancora tu sei, per dirti
ciò che non potevo un tempo — difficile affinità
di pensieri — per dirti, e non ci ascoltano solo
cicale del biviere, agavi lentischi,
come il campiere dice al suo padrone:
« Baciamu li mani ». Questo, non altro.
Oscuramente forte è la vita.

I wanted to speak to you—your parting
signals coloured by the night-time lantern—
to speak to you from this imperfect
wheel of the world,
within a flood of crowded walls,
far from the Arabian jasmine
where you are still, to tell you
what once I could not—difficult
affinity of thoughts—to tell you (not only
the marshland locust, the mastic tree can hear)
as the watchman of the fields tells his master:
«I kiss your hands». This, nothing else.
Life is darkly strong.

Un'anfora di rame

Le spine dei fichidindia
sulla siepe, il tuo corpetto strappato
appena azzurro e nuovo, un dolore
al centro del cuore scavato,
forse a Lentini vicino la palude
di Iacopo notaio d'anguille
e d'amori. Che cosa racconta
la terra, il fischio dei merli
nascosti nel meriggio affamato
di frutta dura di semi
viola e ocra. I tuoi capelli
sulle orecchie in tempesta
che non si svegliano ora, capelli
d'acquarello, di colore perduto.
Un'anfora di rame su una porta
luccica di gocce d'acqua
e fili rossi d'erba.

A Copper Amphora

The thorns of the Indian fig
on the hedge, your bodice—
new and azure—torn, a pain
at the centre of your hollowed heart,
perhaps at Lentini, near the swamp
of Iacopo, the notary
of eels and loves. What does the earth
recount, the whistle of the blackbirds
hidden in the noontime hungry
for fruit that's hard with violet
and ochre seeds. Your hair
over your ears where tempest droned
that now do not awake, your water-
colour hair, its tarnished tone.
A copper amphora on a door
glistening with water drops
and red threads of grass.

Dalla natura deforme

Dalla natura deforme la foglia
simmetrica fugge, l'àncora piú
non la tiene. Già inverno, non inverno,
fuma un falò presso il Naviglio.
Qualcuno può tradire
a quel fuoco di notte, può negare
per tre volte la terra. Com'è forte
la presa, se qui da anni, che anni, guardi
le stelle sporche a galla nei canali
senza ripugnanza, se ami qualcuno
della terra, se scricchiola
il legno fresco e arde la geometria
della foglia corrugata scaldandoti.

Crooked Nature

Now the symmetrical leaf has fled
crooked nature, the anchor cannot
hold her any longer. Now winter, not winter,
a bonfire smokes near the Naviglio.
At that nocturnal fire, someone
can betray, deny—three times—
the earth. How strong the grip must be
if here for years—what years!—you watch
the soiled stars afloat in the canals
without repugnance, if you love
someone on this earth, and if
the fresh wood crackles, the wrinkled leaf's
geometry can blaze, to warm you.

Un arco aperto

La sera si frantuma nella terra
con tuono di fumo e l'assiolo
batte il tu, dice solo
il silenzio. Le isole alte, scure
schiacciano il mare, sulla spiaggia
la notte entra nelle conchiglie.
E tu misuri il futuro, il principio
che non rimane, dividi con lenta
frattura la somma di un tempo già assente.
Come la schiuma s'avvinghia
ai sassi, perdi il senso dello scorrere
impassibile della distruzione.
Non sa la morte mentre muore
il canto chiuso del chiú, tenta intorno
la sua caccia d'amore, continua
un arco aperto, rivela la sua
solitudine. Qualcuno verrà.

An Open Arch

With a roar of smoke, the evening falls
to fragments in the earth, the owl
strikes its "tu," uttering only
silence. And the high, dark islands
crush the sea, upon the sands
night invades the conch shells. You
measure the future, the beginning
already gone, divide—with slow
breaking—the sum of a time now absent.
As the spume of the sea coils round the stones,
you lose the sense of the impassive
flow of the destruction.
While death dies it does not know
the closed song of the owl, it tries
its hunt for love, continuing
an open arch, revealing
its solitude. Someone will come.

Dante

Until now, our century has disclosed to us only a "subterranean" Dante. This, despite the fact that historical and aesthetic criticism, philology and philosophy, have confronted the poet who took apart and then made whole an inexhaustible universe. The questions addressed to Dante's music and lament have scanned the earth and then the heavens, from physical to moral topography. And Dante has been present in the heart of man, with a place there that is constant and not casual. Dante scholars have followed his shadow from the banks of the Arno, through his missions and his exile, and beyond the Alps, which Cino da Pistoia had passed with "grieving voice." The "fullness" of the poet—from the sensuous ferment of his words and their objective correlative (his images, wrested from the realm of the *dolce stil nuovo*'s similes) to the clash of proper names, risen again, through political passion, out of his "sorrowing mind"—has enabled us to reconstruct not only the history of his poetic and spiritual syntax, but that of the Christian and Catholic Middle Ages and of the pagan world, and the relations of these opposing civilizations.

I say a "subterranean" Dante, because neither philological science nor simple or allegorical exegesis have succeeded in making him a part of the scattered culture of today. The Italians, and I should say the Latins—the poets, naturally—

have left him in exile from that day on which "the magnanimous knight [Guido da Polenta] had the dead body of Dante adorned with poetic ornaments on a funeral bier; and had this carried on the shoulders of his most solemn citizens to the place of the Franciscans in Ravenna." [Boccaccio.]

A subterranean Dante and a dead Dante: both, rough figures in a time of waiting. But men like Dante cannot remain interred forever in their tombs. It is not through love or memmory that we elect them, from time to time, contemporary citizens of the world; it is the crisis of a culture, the tortuous corruption of poetic forms and language that makes us turn to them; just as Dante himself once turned to Virgil, the English to Shakespeare, the French to Villon, Racine, Baudelaire.

Today, the decadence of Christian culture is under way; and neither a Crusade against the Albigenses, nor the *Little Flowers* of St. Francis, nor the *Mirror of True Penitence*, nor a new *Summa Theologica*, nor a new pronouncement à la Boniface VIII on the supremacy of religion in the government of this earth—can halt this process. It is only as technique and form that Christian culture endures; for man, from the time of the Enlightenment on, through the empires, historical materialism, dictatorships, the rise of science ("in much wisdom is much pain"), the wars of annihilation, has learned to avoid metaphysical systems and to interrogate himself as a unity linked to other unities. His soul has scrutinized philosophies more rooted in earth than in heaven; and not through scorn or agnosticism, but out of his desire for a forthright analysis of his own consciousness and his unconscious. A man deprived of dreams, who considers his own physical and moral structure "here, on this low shore of the world," comforted by the sole certainty of having to vanish in his dust, can no longer contemplate the divine. Man's shapeless destiny, his uneasiness at the unjust sequence of his days—these warn him that solitude is a precocious version of death. The rhetoric of duties can only torment itself in trying to propose a rebirth of ethical values (*Asperges me*) through abstract deviations from the law—law which has been achieved through the centuries with hostile and fraternal blood. Today, neither a neoclassicism nor a neoromanticism can be born in battered Europe, through new attempts of lances and mercenaries, of reforms and hopes of counter-reform. And whoever dreams of a new Humanism, would have arts and letters turn to the mirage of metamorphoses or to a minor season of imitation. Humanism can mean only one thing today: the condition of man confronted with the still unanswered questions of his life. The relevance of Dante is not incidental, as we shall see. The most recent chapter of European history was written at a time when rhythmic and verbal decorum were exhausted, and the intimate quality of the epigones of the nineteenth century worn out. It has continued to dictate solitude and resignation and indifference, with or without song. The early masters of modern poetry were the heralds of decadence. But in Italy, where criticism also insisted on the name of Leopardi, one found a thinning-out in the body of lyric poetry, and a contorted Petrarchan murmur. A Petrarch, however, not "earned," as had been Leopardi's Petrarch: an Alexandrine Petrarch of the centuries that lay inert, weighed down, from nation to nation, by Marinism, Gongorism, or Euphuism.

Today, we can follow almost with certainty the evolution of Dante's poetic career. I shall not undertake to trace the mutations of his poetics, crowded with emblems and allegories, up to his conquest of the "real," or better, of the transcendental by means of the real. I shall, rather, try to give some sense of his true "book of memory," Dante's search for a center around which his circle of men and shadow and "substances" was to revolve.

Born at the rise of the Signorias, in the dissolving society of the Communes, in the city whose men "are valiant in arms, proud and quarrelsome; a city rich with unlawful gains, and on account of its greatness, distrusted and feared, rather than loved, by the neighboring towns," [Dino Compagni] Dante gathers up the culture of his time, the soaring dreams of the mystics of the universal, the *Tesoro* of Brunetto Latini, seeking approval for his first poems from his contemporary masters and poets. These early writings of his, echoing schemes worn out by the Provençal and Sicilian poets and by intense practice in the vulgar tongue, develop until the death of Beatrice. The *Vita Nuova* will be his first search for order in the alphabet of courtly love, a working-out of the will to silence in his soul that has watched the death of

la gentil donna, che per suo valore
fu posta dall' altissimo Signore
nel ciel dell' umiltate . . .

Vita Nuova, XXXV

["the gentle lady, who for her worth was placed by the most high Lord in the heaven of humility . . ."]

and, finally, a liberation from the *stil nuovo*'s lofty chronicle of the intelligence.

The *Consolations of Philosophy* had been a memorable model for the *Vita Nuova;* but surely only a model of structure, because Dante concludes with the consolation of poetry, whereas Boethius, in his dialogue with philosophy, rejects the verses of sentiment (attached as they are to fame and worldly power) to proceed towards divine truth, the final resolution of human thought. If we consider, at this point, the judgment of the Florentine men of letters on the early verse of Dante, we should say that the praise of the spiritualist Cavalcanti will have less critical relevance for the future poet of the *Comedy* than the harshness of the realist Dante da Maiano.

The *Vita Nuova* is a departure from reality, a deepening of medieval visions; the allegory remains only allegory—it does not move beyond the sense of a preordained representation. So much so, that the human figure of Beatrice becomes dubious amid the innumerable relations between the visible and the invisible. The present penetrates the past with a meditation on ornate gentleness, precisely because this early book of memory has its origins in an "invented" time. Abstract knowledge—and the "pure" poetry of Dante is an intellectual exercise on the emblems of appearances—cheats man of his most certain meaning. Dante weeps with literary resignation; the disciple of Guido Guinizelli, the admirer of the Provençal Arnaut Daniel who was "a better craftsman in the vulgar tongue," here tries out his poetic in dreaming of the death of Beatrice (later, psychoanalysis will dissect the Prophets and the visions): "And I seemed to see the sun grow dark, so that the stars showed themselves of a colour that made me judge they were weeping; and it seemed to me that birds on the wing fell dead and that there were great earthquakes. And marvelling at such fantasy and much afraid, I imagined that a certain friend came to tell me: 'Then don't you know? Your wonderful lady has left this world' . . . In this vision, such great humility overcame me through the sight of her, that I called out to Death and said: 'Sweetest Death, come to me, and be not rude; for you must be gentle, having been in such a place! Now come to me, who so desire you: you see I already wear your colour!' " (In this passage there are obvious echoes of the Sicilian school—"*morte villana*," "rude death," Giacomino Pugliese—and of Guido Cavalcanti—"*vede la morte sotto al meo colore*," "he saw death beneath my colour.") And after the astrological and cabalistic games to signify the day and the month and the year of the death of the beloved, Dante returns to lamentation and weeping that contradict themselves in the span of a canzone:

Gli occhi dolenti per pietà del core,
hanno di lagrimar sofferta pena,
sí che per vinti son rimasi omai.
Or s'io *voglio* sfogare lo dolore,
che appoco appoco alla morte mi mena,
convenemi parlar traendo guai.
E perché mi ricorda ch'io parlai
della mia donna, mentre che vivia,
donne gentili, volentier con vui,
non vo' parlare altrui,
se non a cor gentil che 'n donna sia:
E dicerò di lei *piangendo,* pui
che se n'è gita in ciel subitamente,
ed ha lasciato Amor meco dolente.

Vita Nuova, xxxii

["*Sorrowing for my heart's pity, my eyes have suffered such pain in weeping that now they are vanquished.* Now if *I would* give vent to my grief, which little by little brings me to death, *I had best speak lamentingly.* And because I remember that, while she lived, I spoke willingly of my lady to you, gentle ladies, I would not speak to others, only to a gentle heart that be in woman: And *weeping,*

I shall tell of her, since she has passed straightway to heaven and has left Love sorrowing with me."]

A lament "read" by Boccaccio, who, not without irony, colours it with his agile fantasy: "The days were like the nights, and the nights like the days: no hour passed without laments, without sighs, and without an abundance of tears; and his eyes seemed two brimming fountains of spring water, so much so that most people wondered whence he had so much liquid humour to suffice for his weeping."

We must, however, assign a formative value to the prose of the *Vita Nuova.* Together with the prose of the *Convito*, in the difficult descent from the plane of the abstract lyric to the rational plane, it was to modify the poetic language of Dante. Both for Dante and Boccaccio, the point-of-reference for the fusion of scientific and imaginative prose in the vulgar tongue, was the *Novellino*, the collection of tales whose nucleus dates from the late thirteenth century. Through the rigour of his prose, Dante will arrive at a discursive tone in his poetry, at a technique that breaks with the rhymers of the Tuscan school, their voices smoothed by moral and religious phantoms. The allegorical allusions, the ambitious desire for spiritual solitude, will enter later into the substance of the *Comedy*, but only after Dante's language has become concrete and he has reached a harmony of faith and philosophy.

Having concluded the final chapter of his first youthful "Vision" with the angelic assumption of Beatrice, Dante opens the infinite space of his *Rime*—I mean the so-called *Petrose* poems (those addressed to a woman who is likened to a "*bella pietra*," a "beautiful stone"), in which his destiny of a "minor poet" is altered. Beatrice dies in 1290; 1293 marks the putting in order of the *Vita Nuova.* Dante has already fought at Campaldino; he is part of the Florentine government and a political man in the full sense of the word. And while the struggle between the White and Black Guelf factions assumes political form, the poet opposes the interference of Boniface VIII in Florentine territory. No longer wrapped up in sighs of love and of lament ("and to look at him, he almost seemed a savage thing: lean, bearded, and almost utterly transformed from what he used to be"), he again becomes "haughty in spirit and very disdainful . . . strong in all adversities; in one thing only . . . impatient and quarrelsome, that is, in what pertained to political factions." [Boccaccio.] These are qualities confirmed by Villani: "Rather presumptuous and withdrawn and haughty; and almost in the manner of an ungracious philosopher, he knew not how to speak well with laymen . . ."; and noted by Cavalcanti:

> Solevanti spiacer persone molte,
> tuttor fuggivi la noiosa gente.

["You used to be displeased by a crowd, you always fled from tedious men."]

In the clamour of civil war, Dante resumes his readings of Statius, Ovid, Virgil, Horace, and the philosophical and theological speculation that is to orient him in Thomism. Through his study of the classic poets, Dante will pass beyond the lyric current of rhetoric in the vulgar tongue, with its conventional sentiment. The "drama" had reappeared in the form of the "laud" as a kind of Platonism with the cross: in it, one heard the outcry of condemned nature, *summae Deus clementiae*, "God of the highest mercy." Dante will again people the drama with human figures; and his poetic history will be determined by the motives for song to be found in the revelations of his intellect and by the moral and political pressures on him.

Meanwhile, close to Gemma Donati, the woman he was later to marry, he writes the *Petrose*. From angelic love he turns to the irreducible senses; his mind does not descend to inferior things, but touches—with its image—the most sure and certain realms of beauty. And there he finds a woman hard as stone. We are on the threshold of the *Comedy*, the achievement of personality, the shifting creative urge is about to find its center. The technique of the *Petrose* makes use of words so that they have an almost physical weight; the senses involve the real history, the truth of man (man still not, however, a dramatic figure). There is no liturgical mediation or inauthentic rhetoric in these poems, but thought at last disarmed by love in motion.

Learned poetry, in whose body wisdom is carnal and violent, and solitude, wounded:

Egli alza ad ora ad or la mano, e sfida
la debole mia vita, esto perverso,
che disteso e riverso
mi tiene in terra, d'ogni guizzo stanco:
allor mi surgon ne la mente strida;
e 'l sangue, ch'e per le vene disperso,
fuggendo corre verso
lo cor che 'l chiama . . .
. . . .
cosi vedess' io lui fender per mezzo
lo core alla crudele, che 'l mio squatra;
poi non mi sarebb'atra
la morte, ov'io per sua bellezza corro!

Canzoniere, Canzone vi, Sez. 3

["Soon he (Love) lifts up his hand, and defies—in his perversity—my weak life; he pins me to the ground, outstretched and overthrown, too exhausted even to stir; then shrieks rise up within my mind, and the blood—scattered through my veins—flees running towards the heart that summons it . . . Would I might see him so cleave the heart's center of the cruel she, who quarters mine; then would death, to which I hasten for her beauty, not be so black to me!"]

Dante is an inflexible craftsman and considers the defeat of Guittone d'Arezzo's poetry a defeat of technique; and for love of far-fetched devices, ambiguous alliterations and evocative formulas, he grants enduring poetic merits to the Provençal Arnaut Daniel. The art of saying has now become a perfect science for Dante. But the *Petrose* move in the realm of truth and the sphere of the contingent; with reference to them, we have word from Boccaccio of an intemperance for physical love in Dante: "Mid so much virtue, so much science, as we have shown above to be in this wonderful poet, lust found ample place, and not only in his youthful years, but even in the years of his maturity."

Man's body brings us close to history, not to aesthetics; but the body will serve Dante as the most conscious medium for the appearance, in the world where he hoped to find escape

> Guido, i' vorrei che tu e Lapo ed io
> fossimo presi per *incantamento*
> . . . .
> e quivi *ragionar* sempre d'amore
>
> *Canzoniere,* Son. vi

["Guido, I would that you and Lapo and I were taken by *enchantment* . . . and there *to discourse* always of love."]

of *this* world, where the "beautiful stone" takes on the colours of the seasons and Dante, earthly and impetuous, cries out:

S'io avessi le belle trecce prese.
che fatte son per me scudiscio e sferza,
pigliandole anzi terza,
con esse passerei vespero a squille:
e non sarei pietoso né cortese,
anzi farei com'orso quando scherza.
. . . .
e poi le renderei con amor pace.
Canzoniere, Canzone vi, Sez. 6

["Had I seized the fair locks, that have become my scourge and lash, laying hold of them before the hour of tierce, I would pass vesper and evening bells with them: and I would not be merciful or courteous, but like a bear when he takes his sport . . . *and then, with love, I'd give her peace.*"]

By now Dante's poetry wanders no longer on the sea of the *stil nuovo* stylists, but treads the earth, encountering man with "his blood and his joints." [*Purg.* xxvi, 57.] Realism, the great poetry of Dante, is born in the *Petrose;* the sentiments are not anagogical, but rise out of the flesh, beaten by true wind and rain and hail. The "discourse on love," the dialectic of his early years, is in the shadows; when it reappears again, in the *Paradiso,* we are already at the journey's end, in the weariness of wisdom and the body. But "in the middle of our life's way," Dante da Maiano or Forese Donati would have placed Dante in the seventh vortex of the *Purgatory*, in the ranks of those who sinned through excess of carnal love, together with Guinizelli and Arnaut Daniel and she "who made herself brutish with the wood fashioned in the form of a beast"; among the souls distant from the dark tempest that roars in the second circle of the *Inferno*, souls that are "*sure of* having, whenever it may be, *a state of peace.*"

In the *Petrose* Dante's poetic truth begins to become concrete; and we shall see where it ends.

We are in 1300 and Dante, man of the "dark wood," is Prior of Florence from June 15 to August 15. His political life, which had lasted seven years, is interrupted in 1301; a necessary experience, lived out among the Popolani and the Magnates and bloody discord. Dante has already enumerated in his mind dramatic figures drawn from Florentine society.

We know little of his life in the house of Gemma Donati, though Boccaccio speaks plainly enough of his domestic sentiments: "Once having left her, who had been given to him to console him in his troubles, he never wanted to come where she was, nor ever permitted her to come where he was." But it was surely before he left that house that Dante continued his trials in poetic discourse, with the texts of Ovid and Statius before him. There was born the idea of his second "Vision," a poem of moral judgment linked to the Christian law, and of redemption achieved in accord with the doctrines of Aquinas.

In order to do violence to his soliloquy, Dante turns from the literary thirteenth century, the science of love, the flashing mysticism, to the pagans, to the myths of Ovid, the rude plastic power of the *Metamorphoses*, that desperate ruin of human forms. He meditates on the realism of Ovid, on the elegiac note of the *Tristia*. (The same exile's sorrow is in the *Comedy*, the same Ovidian cadence in "you shall leave everything you love most dearly.") And from the text of Virgil, Dante learns the movement of his characters, his encounters with souls, the meaning of "dialogue." He learns to distinguish between the impetuous turmoil of feelings and the will of man, and to set forth clearly the world's condition. Virgil becomes for Dante the "Summa" of man: he finds his own aspirations in Virgil's political ideal of the Empire, in the lofty melancholy of Aeneas, in the dreams and the humble works, in the mature harmony between poetic content and artistic perfection. "Lettered" Dante will choose as his master the most lettered and the greatest of the Latin poets. Virgil steers him away from the poetic of memory to the poetic of the real, of objects: from allusion to concreteness, from the salutation of courtly woman to invective.

All of philosophy had sought God, considering man—outside his intellect necessary for speculation—a body weighed down with duties. Man, born to pain and death, could annul these in the contemplation of the divine, in achieving the joy of the kingdom of God, sole site of peace and justice. Dante shatters the mysticism and finally finds man; no longer a shifting, makeshift form (the sentiment of the *stil nuovo* poets) but body and intelligence, worthy to begin a dialogue with religious and earthly truth.

Dante's conception and his political action impel the *Comedy* beyond the medieval "allegories" that were pacified in the faith with the fire of anonymous souls cast into the shadows. And we might have had, instead, the Sixth Book of the *Aeneid* made arid by sinners dragged up from the populace, a Sixth Book widened into the dimensions of the Elysian fields! That book of Virgil that sees Homeric Avernus shrill with the shades of heroes (there is the parallelism of the Sybil and Virgil in the *Comedy*, but the branch with golden leaves is a mythical talisman, for the descent to the other world, not to be found in the flora of the Christian paradise):

Ibant obscuri sola sub nocte per umbram
. . . .
quale per incertam luce sub luce maligna
est iter in silvis. . . . .
. . . . . .et rebus nox abstulit atra colorem.
Bk. VI, v. 268-ff.

["They moved along in darkness through the shadow beneath the lonely night . . . as is the journey in the woods under the meager light of a fitful moon . . . and black night stole the colour from things."]

(The invention and the music of Dante's gentle evocations—dawn and twilight and evening's coming—are echoes of Virgilian tones and silences.)

Heroes. In the Middle Ages, heroes slept in their tombs with the ruin of the Roman Empire. The memory of Dante, however, swarmed with men that were to be judged, but not by any prefixed scheme: every moment is a dramatic moment in which there participate freely the law of God, Christian pity, and the life of man. Poetry cannot be chronicle, even if there cry out within it moral judgments suggested by factional politics, or offences and prophecies. Nor is it history, or religious knowledge, or an encyclopedia. In order to reach the heaven of Beatrice and the light of God, Dante had to descend again into the underworld and, through the fiction of allegories, visit the shades in the space assigned to them by the superior will. To gain possession of poetry, he had to pass by way of man; for the Inferno is the place of man in his contradictory nature, of the heart of clay pounded by passions and the tempestuous dreams of the sinning intelligence.

This is the time of exile. Dante has already composed seven

cantos of the *Comedy*, this time a solitary writing. The man of factions no longer reads to other poets his secret science of new forms, of dramatic figures at last, and not of sentiments alone; of things, not allusions to things. Dante sees his poetic world moving on an ideal stage. There he is both spectator and voice in the dialogue, encountering men (shadows, both for his faith and the popular faith) detached from time, vibrant, stormy, writhing in their anguish. Seen from exile, Florence appears to him as his celestial homeland. And it will not be political wrath that decides the fate of his adversaries, assigning them to night or light, but his love of justice, even though Giovanni Villani cautiously lets us know that Dante "took much delight in that *Comedy* in scolding and bawling out, in the guise of a poet, perhaps in part more than should be done: but maybe his exile made him do this."

Maybe his exile. And how many poets have been in exile; those who "scold and bawl out" are always, in history, on the shore of those disturbed by wrongs; on the other shore, instead, sage power has ruled the world!

This other companion of Ovid writes of himself: "Truly I was a ship without sails or rule, driven to various ports and estuaries and shores by the dry wind that parches sorrowful misery." But Francesca, Ulysses, Ugolino, Manfred, are not "politics"; and other names will issue from his burning heart, Capaneo, Farinata, Celestino, the proud and the cowardly, and then the barrators, the fraudulent, those guilty of simony: the complete human nature of the defeated and confused, accepted or not by mercy.

This is a part of that subterranean Dante of whom I spoke at the beginning. The other part (which aesthetic criticism has judged with much favor), the Dante who rises again towards his destiny of Medieval man, towards the heavens where one finds "the number nine"—the Beatrice of his youthful anxieties, the woman touched by Grace because she is free of the rending of the senses, the anti-Francesca—the other part of Dante is not to be identified with great poetry. The *Paradiso* is a flight towards a known place, a return to the *Vita nuova*:

> Paríemi che 'l suo viso ardesse tutto
> e li occhi aveva di letizia si pieni,
> che passar men convien sanza costrutto.
>
> *Paradiso,* xxiii, 22–24

["It seemed to me her face was all aglow, and her eyes so full of gladness that I must pass it by, undescribed."]

a capitulation to culture: the geometry of its technique will not be enough to win out over its aridity, to restore to the objective field the abstract figurations of the intelligence here at work on conditioned matter. The science, the philosophy, the theology remain such, even if they are enunciated in the harmony and measure of this choral canticle. Here the voice of Dante becomes that of a student; not a student of the Muses, as was Virgil:

> Me vero primum dulces ante omnia Musae,
> quarum sacra fero ingenti percussus amore,
> accipiant, caelique vias et sidera monstrent . . .
>
> *Georgics* ii, 475

["More dear to me than anything, may the Muses—whose sacred rites I celebrate, moved by immense love—receive me, and teach me the path of heaven and the stars . . ."]

but a student of God, following the principles of Aquinas. In the eighth heaven of the fixed stars, the poet seems a novice dedicated to Christian doctrine: he undergoes an examination on the three theological virtues from Peter, James, and John, uncommon masters, surely. And the praises Dante receives in the luminous, resounding air, tell us that his ardour is of an intellectual, not a poetic nature.

Through consummate literary technique, the word of Dante (the *Paradiso*, too, has concrete language and the obscurity, if any, is of a spiritual and scientific nature) seeks by itself, its tonal expression. Here, however, the limit is contemplation, negative life, a state of voluntary inertia, a return to the most ardent medieval mysticism. In this canticle is the Middle Ages, with its Church little disposed to experimental knowledge. Speaking to men, the poet had enlarged the world of the culture of his time; speaking of the heavens, he has again circumscribed it. It is one thing to move among corruptible hearts, another to eat "the bread of the angels" without uncertainties, to kneel down and adore in a realm made perfect through the great silence of the immortal dead. Yet we shall remember Dante the man at the point of his redemption, in the quiet of his spirit, as he appears in the utterance of his supreme ecstasy. He had already reached the *Paradiso*, but his "political" heart had resisted the violence of the times. In the contemplation of God he does not forget the earth, if Boccaccio can write these words on the final period of his life: "And what I am most ashamed of, in serving his memory, is that it is a thing well known to all in Romagna that any slip of a girl, any little boy who spoke of factions and damned the Ghibellines, could move him to such fury that he would have thrown stones at them had they not shut up; and he lived with this animosity until his death."

The cult of Dante endures in Italy because of the poet's approach to God through the intellect; the cult of Shakespeare endures instead in England because of the continuous clash in him between the heavens and the earth, that is to say, for his poetry alone. I speak of a cult; because Dante is very great, unique, in the freedom and truth of his language.

Eliot, in his essay on Dante, writes that the *Comedy* can only be compared to the entire body of Shakespeare's work; an unusual acknowledgment, this, for a writer in the English language. The "subterranean" Dante emerges again when studied by the poets. Ezra Pound draws near to him, guided by Cavalcanti; a singular Dante, however, an obscure cipher of hidden meanings and allusions. The language of Pound and Eliot is not the visual and concrete language of Dante: another tradition and the impossibility of their assailing the image directly, restrict these two poets to the zone of learned poetry. "Learned poetry," when they want to make their symbols dense or to construct metaphysics, because in the epic—the term is very approximate—their will to narrate draws them to the schematic, to the diary of the world, to the weary gesture of shadows under feeble light.

Here and there *The Waste Land* has verses of Dante, never Dantesque verses. In the steep images of the poem there are layers of cultural echoes, of distant civilizations, and a funereal, arid air: a world of the living who are dead. In Dante's *Inferno* it is the dead who are alive. Dante's lesson for Eliot could only be one; a lesson of language, of poetry. Instead, the praise that Eliot bestows on the *Paradiso* and the *Vita Nuova* would justify the difficult theology of the English poet, its allegory frozen into a metaphorical meaning only; hermetic wisdom in a poetry that strives for drama and, we said, the epic.

Drama and epic are the aspirations of the new generation

in approaching its moral sorrow. Today, in the silence of Italian poetry, in the "art badly learned" of the imitators, a return to the realistic word of Dante can set aside blurred, baroque Petrarchism. Sentiment should breed human figures; analogies, the relief of powerful images.

Eliot reads Dante with amazement: "The language of Dante is the perfection of a common language." Yet the "simple style," of which Dante is the greatest master, is a very difficult style.

Poscia che fummo al quarto dí venuti,
Gaddo mi si gettò disteso a' piedi,
dicendo: "Padre mio, ché non m'aiuti?"
Quivi morì; e come tu mi vedi,
vid'io cascar li tre ad uno ad uno,
tra 'l quinto dí e 'l sesto; ond'io mi diedi,
già cieco, a brancolar sovra ciascuno;
e due dí li chiamai, poi che fur morti;
. . . .

Inf. xxxiii. 67–74

["When we had come to the fourth day, Gaddo threw himself down, stretched out at my feet, saying: 'My father, why don't you help me?' There he died: and just as you see me, I saw the three fall one by one between the fifth day and the sixth; then I began, already blind, to grope over each, and for two days I called out to them, after they were dead . . ."]

A difficult style; and it is the language of great poetry, beginning with Homer. This language has sung the heavens and the earth; it is the "reality" of man, his life in the signs that reveal it.

The new generation knows that to find man it need not thrust beyond into the inferno: the inferno is here.